50 plus one

Tips When Hiring & Firing Employees

by
**Linda M. Magoon &
Donna de St. Aubin**

Information to Encourage Achievement

1261 West Glenlake
Chicago, IL 60660
www.encouragementpress.com

ISBN: 1-933766-03-4
EAN: 978-1-933766-03-4

This product is not intended to provide legal or financial advice or substitute for the advice of an attorney or advisor.

10 9 8 7 6 5 4 3 2 1
♻ printed on recycled paper

©2007 Encouragement Press, LLC
1261 West Glenlake
Chicago, IL 60660

Special discounts on bulk quantities of Encouragement Press books and products are available to corporations, professional associations and other organizations. For details, contact our Special Sales Department at 1.253.303.0033.

About the Authors

Linda M. Magoon has been a retirement planning specialist and human resource manager for nearly 25 years. Her experience includes both for-profit and non-profit organizations. She has been advising employees and managers on medical and retirement benefits, including both qualified and non-qualified plans, through company-sponsored training programs and seminars.

She has a Masters Degree in Educational and Business Management and currently works for a suburban Chicago school system. In addition to her full-time work, she is teaching business classes on the graduate school level. She is the co-author of *50 plus one Tips to Building a Retirement Nest Egg* (Encouragement, 2007)

Donna de St. Aubin has human resource and management expertise that spans more than 25 years and includes executive human resource positions in the health care, manufacturing, financial and insurance industries. In addition to her experience in human resource management, planning and internal staffing, Ms. St. Aubin has also been involved in major corporation mergers, acquisitions, divestitures and consolidations. She develops and conducts executive management workshops and works frequently with companies in health care, pharmaceuticals, manufacturing and service organizations. Her understanding of business cultures as well as the intricacies of organizational designing and development has enabled her to create programs that effectively position private and public companies for continued growth. She works with individual executives in coaching and mentoring along with teams and organizations.

Acknowledgements

Special thanks…and cheers to the following:

Maris Feinberg and Jen Fester

Table of Contents

Firing

Introduction

I have always hired the right person, except when I did not–
and then I knew it almost immediately.

Never were truer words spoken. Getting the right people, keeping the best people and letting go unsuitable employees is both frustrating (when it is not right) and very gratifying (when it does work). You can never be quite sure, no matter how much time and effort is spent, if you have the right person for the right job.

Whether your business is large or small, for profit or not, the single most important decisions you make are about the employees you hire (or fire, for than matter). Even the most experienced managers and business owners make mistakes from time to time, which is both personally very frustrating and terribly expensive. Of course, mistakes are more than just money, but opportunity costs, poor department or company morale and the ever-present risk of lawsuits.

How do you improve the odds that you will make the rights decisions concerning employees? *50 plus one Tips When Hiring & Firing Employees* is an excellent start to learning the complicated, often confusing facts surrounding employee decisions. In succinct, easy-to-understand chapters, just about every facet of hiring and firing is discussed for business owners and general mangers to use with confidence.

Hiring is not only an issue of finding the right person for the right job, but it is very much about following the laws–and they are extensive–to make sure that you and your company are well protected because of possible discrimination and unfair labor practices. The cost of ignorance of the law and poor personnel policies can be hugely expensive–a problem that no one wants to have on their backs!

Be smart, be aware, be positive and most of all be legal by using *50 plus one Tips When Hiring & Firing Employees* as your first, easy-to-use and easy-to-understand basic reference on hiring, firing, employee retention, creating personnel policies and saving money, time and aggravation.

Linda M. Magoon

Donna de St. Aubin

plus one

You Need a Body...
But Not Just Any Body

The Challenge for Every Organization

This book is about hiring and firing employees, and much more. It is about the ultimate success or failure of your enterprise, whether for-profit or not-for-profit. Every company or organization advertises its focus on the people who form and run the enterprise. Every mission statement and almost every social gathering of employees begins with high praise for the people who work for the company, and how it would be impossible for the company to succeed without these very employees.

And yet, the first way owners and executives look to cut costs is reducing the head count, by outsourcing or downsizing, or by converting employees from regular to contract status. There is an inherent contradiction in the way we speak and the way we act as managers and supervisors. Few can appreciate the subtle and not so subtle influences that permeate organizations, such that in the long run many employees become unhappy, dissatisfied or unproductive.

In a recent survey taken by a major research organization, thousands of workers were asked how they felt about their jobs. Nearly 60 percent of respondents reported being either burned out or completely exhausted. Their most frequently reported complaints were the sheer amount of work, unrealistic deadlines, unpleasant bosses and difficult co-workers. Time and again workers complain about a lack of loyalty on the part of the company. Time and again, managers complain about a transient work force that has no commitment to the enterprise.

There are very good reasons why labor unions (and craft guilds long before them) were founded; managers and owners failed to keep their side of the employment bargain. Working conditions were terrible; job security was nonexistent; wages were low; and labor had no say in the enterprise. The social and economic contract between labor and management did not work.

Because services comprise such a large percentage of the gross national product, and because the economic environment is now globally oriented, there is tremendous pressure for productivity gains—more and faster work at the same wages and with the same benefits.

Hiring, retaining and firing employees can be so complicated that many managers and owners fail to recognize the importance of these activities. Marketing, new product development, technology and cash management are often the top priorities; but should they be? What fuels successful departments and continuous business development is a stable, productive and dedicated labor force. The organization needs to make proper and legal decisions about hiring and firing— and not just find a body and put him or her to work.

What should be in theory is far different than what happens on a daily basis. Real pressures exist, and hiring and firing is difficult work even when done correctly. This gets back to the basic issue, that is, you need a body because:

- The call center is behind almost every week.
- Two college counselors have taken leaves of absence for the semester.
- Two people have given notice in the accounting department.
- The company is growing and it is simply understaffed.
- Customer service cannot work more overtime.
- The retail product manager is the wrong person for the job.
- The case load in social services is too high.
- The programmer does not have the rights skills to do the work.
- The receptionist is chronically late and absent.

The list goes on and on. People leave, organizational changes take place, or there is simply more work than the current staff can handle. The pool of candidates, in theory, is limitless, but it seems very small. Finding the right people for open positions, despite numerous resources including the Internet, is like finding a needle in a haystack.

Your goal as an owner or a manager is to improve your odds of making the right hiring decisions. Because this book is written for managers and companies that probably do not have a human resource department, it assumes that hiring is done by individuals who are not specialists in interviewing and hiring. These activities are just part of the job.

A Planned Approach to Hiring

Your goal in hiring and personnel decisions should be directed by what is best practice in your industry. Best practice is nothing more than setting standards, or benchmarks, for a particular activity in an organization. You want to establish a standard by which you judge both new and existing employees. Best practice suggests that you develop your standards from what is most successful for a group your size, in your locale, and in your industry.

Many organizations use specific and quantifiable benchmarking criteria, but this is not always practical for small businesses or not-for-profit groups. Even so, you can set down written plans and specifications for hiring and retaining employees. But where do you get information about best practice within your employment sphere? Here are a few suggestions:

- Attend industry- or government-sponsored seminars and learn more about what is common practice. Speakers and attendees can be good information sources.
- Consulting groups and accounting firms often provide help to learn more about benchmarking on their Websites or through free special reports mailed to potential clients.
- Talk to other owners and managers in your own or similar industries. People can be surprisingly forthcoming about their policies and procedures. If you show interest, they want to demonstrate their successes. You can learn a great deal from your peers.
- Speak to current employees who worked for other employers. Ask them to outline best practice at their former company.
- Consider hiring a consultant for a limited term, say 2 or 3 days at the stated rate. Not only might the consultant help with establishing benchmarking, but he or she may be in a position to assist in your overall planning.

Remember your goal is objectivity, not bureaucracy and red tape. Try to approach best practice in a way that fits hiring needs for all departments and levels within your organization. You want to be able to adapt your standards and benchmarks to all positions you will need to fill.

Best Practice Includes Short- and Long-Term Planning

Many experts say that long-term planning is a myth, but there is an important part that is both useful and practical. Whatever your time frame, you and your key employees are trying to understand what your business is now and what it might look like some time in the future. Going beyond a year or two and expecting to be accurate is probably impossible, especially for smaller organizations. So many events can take place that it makes it very difficult to predict. But, you can try to understand what events might have a significant impact on your group:

- Sales and revenue growth or decline
- Success or failure of new products
- Recession

- New government regulations
- Labor market conditions
- Amount of competition
- Loss of a key employee
- New technology or manufacturing
- Outsourcing

Of course, there is no single answer to any of these and other related issues. You may create two or three scenarios that anticipate both positive and negative influences on your organization. This planning is directly tied to your employment needs. In this discussion, you are trying to anticipate what kinds of employees you will hire (or let go) over the next couple of years.

Now draft a specific employment game plan and objectify your employment needs by creating best practice benchmarks. Your criteria may include:

- The total number of employees needed.
- Level of employment: technical (computer programmer), professional (lawyer) or general (customer service).
- Salary levels.
- Benefit packages (not everyone receives stock options, the same vacation time, and so forth).
- Cost of recruitment or incentives (stock options, signing bonus).
- Related work place improvements (new computers, additional offices).
- Adjustments/changes to current salary and benefits for existing employees.

A somewhat jaded example is a consumer loan company with hundreds of small branch offices, each one headed by a branch manager. Because of low pay and poor morale, the company-wide turnover for this position was 116 percent per year. This means that statistically, every branch changed managers once a year, and 16 percent of them twice a year! (Ironically, the company had an excellent training program, making their employees attractive candidates for banks, savings and loans and other lending institutions.) No matter the circumstances, key executives could anticipate their employment needs with a good deal of accuracy.

The Need for Job Descriptions

Once you have identified the number and type of employees you might need over the next 18 months, you need to create specific job descriptions for these positions. This is where the objective, analytical work begins. You are trying to set benchmarks for the work an employee will do, so that you will have a standard to compare candidates for this job.

Job descriptions seem to be only for large companies, and that they are elaborate and lengthy analyses of job duties. Both of these assumptions are not true. Each employee in a small company can have a job description, which may and probably will change as the company grows. If nothing else, job descriptions prevent turf wars, which occur in companies of all sizes. A one-page outline will work nicely:

1. Job title
2. General description of activities
3. Salary range
4. Educational background
5. Related work experience required
6. Technical or computer skills required
7. Supervisory responsibilities, if any
8. To whom this person reports, including an organizational chart (company or department)
9. Other duties as assigned

One caution about job descriptions is that if they are too specific, they tend to stifle individual initiative. If you state that the receptionist's only responsibilities are to greet visitors, answer the phone and keep the reception area tidy, then that is all that employee will want to do. The job description includes these basic responsibilities and well as other duties as time and need suggest (taking overflow calls from customer service, assist with client billing, and so forth). You want your employees to grow professionally and allow for some overlap in abilities in case other employees are absent or leave the company.

With your planning document and job descriptions in hand, you are almost ready to start the hiring process. But one more item is an absolute necessity.

An Employee Manual

You might consider an employee manual above and beyond the needs of a smaller organization. In fact, an employee manual will help you manage, motivate and discipline employees, no matter the size of your company. A typical employee manual would include:

- Company mission statement and history
- Company hours
- Statement on fair and equal employment and promotion
- Policy on sexual harassment
- Amount of time for lunch and breaks
- Drug and alcohol abuse
- Performance reviews
- Promotion policies
- Reasons for termination

- Employee benefits
- Salary administration
- Dress code
- Vacations and company holidays
- Leaves of absence

Make your employee manual simple, specific and accurate. In the future, you may need to defend an employment decision you have made, and your employee manual can support your decision.

Finally, remember that your hiring plan, policy and actions should be fair, ethical and consistent. Take the high road and you will be rewarded with quality employees who will grow with your organization.

The Resources

A number of sites on the Internet sell basic forms and documents for hiring, training, firing and legal compliance. In particular, there are basic templates for employee manuals which are easy to use and can be readily adapted to your company needs–and they are inexpensive. Visit *www.socrates.com* for a ready-to-use employment manual.

You can also purchase a *Hiring Policy Kit*, which includes policies, forms and standard letters, from *www.hrpolicyanswers.com*

1

Knowing the Law When Hiring Employees

Know the Laws

There are general guidelines to follow when hiring employees, whether your organization is large or small. You want to ensure that prospective employees can do their jobs and adapt to the culture and environment in which they will work. You also want to ensure that you abide by all applicable state and federal laws. The following federal laws are important for all who participate in the interview and selection process.

Equal Pay Act of 1963

This law prohibits wage discrimination by requiring equal pay for equal work. Equal work is defined by four elements:

- Equal skills: the experience, training, education and ability required to perform a job.
- Equal effort: the physical or mental exertion needed to perform a job.
- Equal responsibility: the extent to which an employer relies on an employee to perform the job as expected, with an emphasis on accountability.
- Equal working conditions: the physical surroundings and any job hazards, including inside or outside work, excessive heat or cold, and the quality of workplace ventilation.

There are exceptions to this law, including:

- a seniority system
- a merit pay system
- geographic wage differentials
- a real difference in the quality or quantity of expected work output

Immigration Reform and Control Act of 1986

This law prohibits discrimination against applicants on the basis of national origin or citizenship; establishes penalties for hiring illegal aliens; and requires employers to establish each employee's identity and eligibility to work.

Under this law, when hiring, employers with four or more employees may not:

- Discriminate because of national origin against U.S. citizens, U.S. nationals or authorized aliens.
- Discriminate because of citizenship status against U.S. citizens, U.S. nationals, or aliens in the following classes who have work authorizations: permanent residents, temporary residents (i.e., individuals who have gone through the legalization program), refugees, and those seeking asylum.

Employers comply with the law by following the verification requirements on Form I-9, which include:

- Hiring only those individuals who are legally authorized to work in the United States. A U.S. citizen-only hiring policy is generally illegal. However, U.S. citizenship may be a requirement for certain jobs under federal, state or local law, or by government contract.
- Completing Form I-9 for all new hires. This form helps employers establish that their employees are legally authorized to work in the United States.
- Allowing new hires to present any document or combination of documents to confirm their identity and/or employment eligibility. Employers cannot prefer one document over another for purposes of completing the form, because not all authorized aliens carry the same documents. Any documents that are allowed by law and that appear to be genuine should be accepted.

Title VII of the Civil Rights Act of 1964

Title VII prohibits discrimination based on race, color, religion, sex, or national origin. The law transformed American society by outlawing discrimination in public facilities, in government, and in employment. According to the law:

> *It shall be an unlawful employment practice for an employer…to fail or refuse to hire or to discharge any individual, or otherwise to discriminate against any individual with respect to his compensation, terms, conditions, or privileges of employment, because of such individual's race, color, religion, sex, or national origin….*

Title VII governs both the hiring process and the duration of employment. This law sets the stage for additional topics covered in later chapters.

Americans with Disabilities Act of 1990 (ADA)

This law prohibits employment discrimination against qualified individuals with disabilities. A qualified individual possesses the skills, experience and education to perform the essential functions of a job, with or without reasonable accommodation.

To be protected under the ADA, an individual must:

- Have a physical or mental impairment that substantially limits one or more major life activities;
- have a record of such an impairment; and
- be regarded as having such an impairment.

Major life activities are those essentials such as:

- Bathing–the ability to wash oneself.
- Dressing–the ability to dress oneself and attach braces, artificial limbs or devices.
- Toileting–the ability to get to and on and off the toilet and maintaining hygiene.
- Transferring–the ability to get in and out of a chair or bed without equipment.
- Continence–the ability to control elimination functions.
- Eating–the ability to get nourishment.
- Learning–the ability to learn.

An essential function is a primary job duty that a qualified individual must be able to perform. It may be considered essential either because it is a key job requirement or because it is highly specialized. A reasonable accommodation is the modification of a job or a work environment that enables a qualified individual with a disability to perform the job's essential functions.

Employers covered by the ADA must ensure that qualified individuals with disabilities:

- Have an equal opportunity to apply for jobs and to work in jobs for which they are qualified;
- have equal access to future promotions;
- have equal access to benefits and privileges of employment, such as employer-provided health insurance or training; and
- are not harassed because of their disability.

An employer covered by the ADA may not ask a job applicant questions as to:

- His or her physical or mental impairment or the origin of that impairment (e.g., why the applicant uses a wheelchair);
- his or her use of medication; and
- his or her history of workers' compensation claims.

An employer covered by the ADA may ask questions as to:

- Whether the applicant has the right education, training and skills for the position;

- whether the applicant can satisfy the job's requirements or essential functions (describe them to the applicant); and
- the amount of time that the applicant was absent when previously employed (but not the reasons for such absences), why the applicant left a previous job, or the nature of any past disciplinary actions.

You may not require a job applicant to have a medical examination until after you have made a conditional job offer. Should the applicant appear to have a disability, however, you may ask whether he or she will need a reasonable accommodation in the workplace, even before you make a conditional job offer.

In summary, questions or comments designed to elicit information regarding an applicant's race, color, ancestry, age, sex, religion, disability or handicap must be avoided in the hiring process.

The Resources

Consult the EEOC's Website *www.eeoc.gov* for the most current information regarding federal employment law.

2

Job Descriptions

Job Descriptions Define Worker Responsibilities

No matter how large or small your company is, from the CEO on down, everyone in your employment needs a job description. Why are job descriptions so important? Providing a written job description to every employee establishes clear expectations about tasks and responsibilities, and eliminates duplication of effort and finger pointing. In small companies where job functions often overlap, job descriptions provide clear-cut direction to each employee and serve as a benchmark for evaluations, pay increases and bonuses. In larger companies, job descriptions define qualifications and pay scales, and serve as a benchmark for pay increases, bonuses and advancement potential. In any company, job descriptions serve to protect against litigation.

A job description typically outlines the necessary skills, training, and education needed by a potential employee, and lists a job's duties and responsibilities. It can provide a basis for interviewing candidates, orienting a new employee, and evaluating job performance. A well-designed job description simplifies the interview process and informs candidates of a job's requirements. If you know what skills you are looking for, you will have an easier time knowing what questions to ask and identifying which candidates will best fit your open position.

A job description should be reviewed during an employee's performance review to ensure it accurately reflects the job's current duties and responsibilities. Managers should reevaluate job descriptions with their employees, because employees know the work that has been done and that which needs to be done. Human resources professionals should then review the revised description to ensure that it is legally defensible.

Training and development programs help to conform your employees' skills to industry standards. These programs are also used for succession planning or organizational development; for example, what additional skills can an employee acquire to propel the growth of the organization as a whole?

Job descriptions aid in demonstrating compliance with employment laws, most notably the Americans with Disabilities Act (ADA) of 1990. A terminated employee may sue for wrongful discharge. If a company cannot produce even the most basic job description, it will be difficult to prove termination of employment for nonperformance.

Every job description should include the following 15 items:

1. Job title.
2. Job location.
3. Whether the position is exempt or non-exempt according to the Fair Labor Standards Act (FLSA).
4. Financial responsibilities and implications stated in dollars.
5. Summary describing the purpose of the job and why it exists.
6. Listing of specific duties and major responsibilities, especially the essential duties of the job. A task is considered essential if the job exists in order to perform the function. There are is a limited number of people who can perform the duties of a job, and failure to do so can adversely effect the organization. A good way to determine responsibilities is to estimate the number of hours spent in performing a function within a 40-hour week. Estimate a percentage of time each task will take to complete; all percentages should add to 100 percent.
7. Job qualifications, describing the minimum education, experience, and skills necessary to perform the job. Examples: Conditions of employment such as lifting amount in pounds; frequency of bending, stair climbing, kneeling, twisting; environmental considerations such as noise exposure, chemicals, dust.
8. Working conditions, describing work-related hazards and environmental conditions that occur while performing the job and the essentials for safety. Examples: The presence of loud noises; the need to remain on one's feet for long stretches of time; or the amount of protective equipment required. Express physical requirements of the job in concrete, quantifiable terms to avoid tagging a job as gender-specific.
9. The ADA established that essential job functions become a legal standard in order to fight discrimination against people of certain physical impairments.
10. A summary statement, including a general statement of duties and mentions to which the employee would report.
11. Job functions, including daily tasks and any supervisory functions. Indicate whether internal and/or external contact is required.
12. Attributes needed for the position. If the position involves the use of machinery or technology, detail the type of machines or technology the

position requires. Also detail any technical or educational requirements that may be critical or desired. Provide insight into the type of work environment you want to maintain. Is it purely a business environment, or is the person expected to contribute to the organization's overall spirit.

13. Provide details on the reporting and organizational structure. Include the titles of both the immediate supervisor and any direct reports.
14. Define evaluation criteria.
15. Include the range or grade of compensation rather than a specific figure.

The job description should be free from judgments about how well the job is currently performed or what is expected in the future. It may be used as a tool for measuring and establishing further career development, but these items are better addressed in an employee's performance management plan. Job requirements should be tied directly to job demands. Stay objective and nonjudgmental, and never define job specifications with an individual in mind.

Lastly, understand the difference between a job specification and a job description.

- A job specification identifies the skills and abilities needed to perform a job.
- A job description defines the position and describes the job.

Here are eight rules to follow when writing an effective job description:

1. Use clear and concise language.
2. Use nontechnical language whenever possible so that the language is understandable even to a layperson.
3. Avoid unnecessary words.
4. Keep sentence structure as simple as possible. Begin each sentence with an active verb and always use the present tense.
5. Describe the desired outcome of the work.
6. Use generic terms instead of proprietary names.
7. Avoid using gender-based language.
8. Qualify whenever possible.

Descriptions of job titles appear in a variety of forms in the workplace. Recruitment ads, compensation surveys and other benchmarking tools, as well as corporate or departmental development plans all use some method of describing a job.

The Resources

The Internet is a great source of help in crafting a job description.

JobGenie (*www.stepfour.com/jobs/*) lists all job descriptions from the *Occupational Outlook Handbook* (also located at *www.bls.gov/oco/*). There is also a helpful site at *http://iso9k1.home.att.net/jobs/index.html* that focuses on writing job descriptions.

Also visit *www.encouragementpress.com* for a useful job description update form.

Employee Manual

Why Develop an Employee Manual or Handbook?

Generally speaking, all businesses with greater than one employee should develop and implement an employee manual. Some may argue that there is no need for a formal employee manual in a company with fewer than five employees; most experts, however, agree that it is prudent to have a written policy in place regardless of the number of employees. In some states, fair employment and housing laws apply when a company hires its fifth employee. Federal laws governing civil rights, employees with disabilities, and maternity leave apply to companies with a minimum of 15 employees. Having an employee manual will help prevent you from violating these rules and regulations.

An employee manual or handbook, if done properly, protects both the employee and the employer from potential problems. A well-written employee handbook communicates expectations clearly so that employers and employees operate under the same set of rules. By spelling out the company's policies and procedures that govern employee behavior and company culture, an employee manual helps ensure there will be no misunderstandings, and can significantly decrease the company's chance of being sued. An employee manual provides an employer with a forum to communicate important company standards, benefits, terminology and values.

Having an employee manual also saves time both for you and for your human resources staff. Your employee manual should be a document that your employees refer to on their own instead of repeatedly asking the same questions. Employees typically will not do this on their own; you need to be clear that they are to check with the manual before calling or e-mailing the human resources department. An employee handbook also helps you train employees well and provides a road map for the company. Your employees will learn more about your company by seeing its policies and philosophies in one place in a way that standard public relations or marketing brochures cannot.

Updating the manual regularly and checking it to make certain it does not contain any inconsistencies or contradictions is critical to its success. The employee handbook plays an essential role in making certain your employees are all treated fairly and consistently. Supervisors need to know that the rules apply to everyone; they cannot treat one employee different from another without running the risk of serious consequences.

Employment manuals should be available in hard copy format that each employee can keep at his or her desk. If the company has sufficient resources, the manual should also be available electronically either online, typically through a company's Intranet or as a word processing document. This is vital information that needs to be readily accessible to everyone in the company.

While selecting the proper content in your manual is absolutely imperative, you also need to choose the tone carefully. The wording of the handbook is crucial. If the handbook is written in a casual style, it might not be taken seriously. If it is written in an academic tone and is too strict or formal, it may be ignored. Sentences that are clear and to the point are less likely to be misinterpreted or misunderstood. Because the manual often provides the employee with their introduction to the company, it needs to be written in a neutral, professional manner. It is helpful to have more than one person proofread the manual. Each person tends to view information just a bit differently from the next; having multiple reviewers go over the manually carefully increases the clarity and comprehension of your handbook.

One danger in developing an employee manual that needs to be considered is the possibility that information will be inadvertently left out or not written clearly. These mistakes should be avoided at all costs as they can drastically increase the chances of litigation. An issue that is addressed incompletely or with room for interpretation can cause major problems for the company. This is why it is critical to be as thorough and complete as possible considering all types of situations. The guidelines below cover general and specific issues to address. You can also use templates put out by established, reputable human resources or law firms to aid you in building the appropriate manual for your company. The manual should always be checked by legal counsel before you distribute it company-wide.

The Challenge

Providing Comprehensive Written Guidelines for Employment

Many manuals begin with a brief history of the company. An introduction can also contain background information about the company as well as the company's philosophy, culture, purpose and goals. Placing a table of contents at the front of the manual is desirable. Many employee manuals also contain an index at the back, but this is optional.

Guidelines for Developing an Effective Employee Manual

Tantamount to creating a comprehensive, effective employee manual is understanding that the employee is entitled to know what is expected of him or her. No one likes to be surprised. Spell out expectations and responsibilities. This is for your benefit as well as your employees. While you need not include every possible situation, you need to be clear concerning the following policies and procedures:

1. Employment policies including an explanation of at-will employment versus contract employment.
2. Attendance policy addressing:
    a. Hours of attendance and work;
    b. flextime policy if available; and
    c. summer hours if applicable.
3. Time off policies, which typically include:
    a. Holidays;
    b. vacations;
    c. sick leave;
    d. personal days;
    e. occasional absence days;
    f. short- and long-term disability;
    g. Family Medical Leave Act (FMLA);
    h. military leave;
    i. jury duty; and
    j. workers' compensation.
4. Compensation and salary structure, including:
    a. The difference between exempt and non-exempt employees;
    b. overtime guidelines; and
    c. comp time guidelines.
5. Employee development and behavior policies, including:
    a. Performance appraisals;
    b. promotions;
    c. disciplinary action;
    d. dress code, both summer and winter;
    e. confidentiality and privacy;
    f. recruitment and employee referrals;
    g. internal applications;
    h. discrimination;
    i. harassment;
    j. drug, alcohol, weapon, and workplace violence; and
    k. voice mail, e-mail, and Internet communications; and building safety.

Policies that focus on specific company benefits should also be spelled out. This can either be within the employee handbook or in a completely separate packet. This information must be updated at least once a year to reflect the new health benefits and pricing structure. These include:

- Health, dental and vision policies;
- life and accident insurance policies;
- flexible spending account policies: this can include day care, health care and commuter spending;
- memorial/life events contribution policies;
- 401(k) or other employee saving plan policies;
- pension plan policies; and
- service awards policies.

When to present the handbook is up to you. Many small companies hand out the manual on an employee's first day. Some larger companies choose to present their employee manual at the time of orientation. They find it valuable to go through the manual with new employees almost page by page so there is no misinterpretation. If you decide to go this route, it is may be more efficient to wait until you have a few employees, but do not wait too long.

Finally, make certain that there is a place in the manual where the employee can indicate that he or she read and understands the stated policies. The employee should either sign and date a hard copy document or send an electronic confirmation. This vital step cannot be overemphasized or ignored. Your employee handbook does no one any good if it is not read. All your research and carefully chosen words will be meaningless if your target audience, namely your employees, do not read what you have written. Also, you can have the most thorough, well-written manual, but if you cannot prove that the employee in question read and accepted your policies, you will have a difficult time defending your case in a court of law.

When you hire an employee, your goal is usually to create and maintain a strong employer-employee relationship. Providing and using a complete, well-written employee manual is an important step in fostering the environment you need to make your employees work hard for you.

The Resources

There are many electronic templates and software programs available for purchase that can help you write a comprehensive, understandable employee handbook.

General sites that can be helpful when compiling an employee manual include *www.alllaw.com*, *www.toolkit.cch.com* and *http://humanresources.about.com*.

Using People to Find People

Preparing to Start the Search

Everyone knows that it is often difficult to find a job. Most people have been unemployed at some point in their lives, and they understand the stress and tension involved in the job search. But finding the right employee is often difficult as well. Most employers spend a considerable amount of time and money in finding candidates to interview and hire.

Determining that you have a position to fill is typically the first step. This situation normally arises when you need to replace a terminated employee or one who has resigned. You may also decide to hire someone when the needs and desires of a particular department necessitate additional staff. You may also need to hire from outside the company if another position is filled from within.

This is the perfect time to take stock. You and your staff need to review the qualifications that your future employee must have. It is strongly recommended that you start by analyzing the position's job description line-by-line, if not word-for-word. You should ensure that the job description accurately reflects the job's current duties. Clarity is critical; do not be afraid to add, change or remove requirements. To find the perfect person for the vacancy, you need to know the skills and experience your employee needs.

Once you have ascertained that the job description accurately describes the position you are trying to fill, you need to get the word out. There might be rare instances where you already have resumes of qualified candidates already on hand, but in most cases, you will be starting from scratch. There are many ways to begin your search. This chapter will concentrate on using paid professionals to find the right employees. Chapter 5 addresses the correct methods for using print and other media effectively to find employees.

Employment Agencies

Employment agencies are often used by companies that have little or no time to devote to finding and interviewing viable candidates. Many companies use employment agencies exclusively; others use them occasionally, where there is insufficient time to devote to the hiring process. If you have not established a relationship with a reputable employment agency, spend the time to find a good match for you and your company. Do not choose an employment agency in haste.

Most employment agencies are staffing and recruiting firms that typically handle low- or mid-level positions. These firms charge a fee to the employer when one of their clients is hired; this is known as contingency recruitment. These agencies often have a specific industry focus, such as retail or accounting. These specialty firms target their advertising to reach people interested in these types of jobs, and tend to tailor their searches for qualified personnel to fit their niche market. Their expertise in finding qualified employees in these fields makes them an ideal choice for companies who do not want to spend the time weeding out poorly qualified candidates. Many agencies offer a trial or probationary period for an employee, meaning that the agency will provide a replacement or refund your payment if the employee they recommended is not a good fit. If your company is looking for a mid-level or lower employee, a local employment agency may be your best bet. Adecco Staffing and Paige Personnel are examples of this kind of employment agency.

Some employment agencies charge a fee to the job seeker as well as the hiring firm, but this is uncommon. Agencies affiliated with non-profit groups such as Catholic Charities might request a donation if you hire their candidate, but they do not typically charge an up-front fee. Be especially leery of any agencies that charge the person seeking employment.

Recruitment Firms/Headhunters

Another type of employment agency is a recruitment firm, or a headhunter. These are executive search firms that usually find company officers and executives. Highly paid attorneys, physicians, and others who earn upwards of $100,000 fall into this category. Headhunters either specialize by geographic location or the type of employee needed. These agencies usually receive an up-front retainer fee in addition to a percentage of the employee's salary and bonus if their candidate is hired.

Headhunters conduct research to appropriately match candidates to companies. This is a time consuming process. The retainer is payment for this research and can be as high as 33 percent of the executive's starting salary. The retainer is paid out in thirds: the first third is paid initially, and the remainder is paid 30 and 60 days after the first day of employment, respectively. If you are looking for a high-end executive, use this type of employment agency, but you must make your requirements crystal clear. You will pay a fair amount of money for a recruitment firm's expertise and you do not want to spend it in vain.

Temporary Agencies

Temporary agencies match individuals who seek short-term temporary work with companies that need periodic extra help. Temporary employees usually do not receive benefits and are ineligible for paid time off, so companies can hire them at a considerable cost savings. Temporary work can also be a foot in the door with a company, which often works to the benefit of both the employer and the employee. An employer that hires a temporary worker for a permanent full-time job already knows that employee's work habits and potential, and the employee will have more job security. In these cases, the employer may have to pay an additional fee to the agency, but this amount is usually small compared to the amount spent in a more traditional search. Temporary agencies are typically paid twice the actual hourly rate for the position, and this arrangement lasts the duration of the assignment. The temporary agency must handle any problems that the employee encounters on the job, and answers employee questions on matters such as salary and time off.

No matter which route you choose, finding the right kind of employment agency to help you find the right employee requires research. Good employees are vital to the success of your business. Do not short-change yourself when looking to hire new employees.

The Resources

Your best sources for employment agencies are friends and business associates who have taken advantage of agency services. You can also search the Website of the Better Business Bureau, *www.bbb.com* for information on reputable agencies. The Headhunters Directory *www.beadbuntersdirectory.com* allows you to search for agencies using a map interface.

5

Using Media to Find People

How to Make Print Advertising and the Internet Work for You

Once the most common method of finding employees, newspaper classified ads, are now viewed as only one tool in a stable of resources. Various surveys and studies have put the success rate for finding employees through newspaper classified ads alone at less then 5 percent. Clearly, this is not an effective way of spending your hiring dollars. Fortunately, other methods, often used in tandem with newspaper and magazine ads have a much better success rate. Not too surprisingly, it is the Internet that has significantly changed how potential employees find work and how companies fill their positions.

The six most common types of media used to find employees:

1. Classified or display ad placed in a large urban newspaper, i.e. the Chicago Tribune.
2. Classified or display ad placed in a trade magazine.
3. Classified ad placed in a small suburban newspaper.
4. Classified ad placed on a general job site such as Monster.com or Careerbuilder.com.
5. Classified ad placed on a specialized job Website such as healthjobsonline.com.
6. Placing open positions on your own company Website.

There are ways to make your search more successful. Because the cost of placing advertisements is a burden on any budget, you will want to make sure you are getting the best bang for your buck. Using the right words and placing your ad in the right place will significantly increase your chances of finding qualified candidates quickly. No company has the time or the money to waste when it comes to finding employees; you need to get it right the first time.

Tips for Using Your Print Advertising Budget Wisely

Write What You Mean

No matter which methods you employ in your quest for employees, the key to finding the right person is how you compose your ad. What you say in the small space you have to describe the position is critical. If you need a cheerful, bubbly receptionist, say so. If you are looking for a serious number cruncher who needs to stay on task day and night, put it in writing. If you place a display or classified ad in your city's major newspaper, you will likely be flooded with resumes. You do not want to waste your time sifting through hundreds of resumes. By carefully writing your ad, you will increase your chances of receiving resumes from bona fide candidates, which will save you time and money in your search.

Place Your Ad Carefully

General/Targeted Publication

Once you write the copy for your ad, you need to decide where to place it. This should be taken into account as you are creating the ad, but a definite decision must be made once the ad is written. You need to consider whether the ad should be placed in a general interest publication, such as a newspaper, or whether it is specific enough to be run in a trade magazine or journal. Many professions, including electricians, plumbers, carpenters, health care workers, lawyers, and publishers have magazines. If your company is in a particular field, the decision will be easier. The call is not as clear if you are looking for someone outside your area. Then the question becomes whether qualified candidates are likely to find you in a general publication or a publication targeted to their field.

Trade publications are typically published less frequently than a newspaper and will charge you more to advertise with them. You must decide whether it is worth the additional cost in both time and money to target your ad directly. You also have to select the publication in which to place your ad in if there are competing journals in the field in which you are looking. While many newspapers have online sites as well, placing an ad in their print version does not necessarily entitle you to an online ad unless that is stated in your contract.

Local/National/International Publication

If you decide to advertise in the newspaper and not a trade magazine, you still have decisions to make. Will you place your ad in a publication that reaches many readers, such as the Chicago Tribune or New York Times, or will you advertise in smaller scale publications? Among the factors to consider in this decision are your actual physical location and the salary you plan to pay. If you are located in a small town and need a larger applicant pool, then the paper with the larger, broader circulation would seem to be the right choice. If your needs are not specific and you cannot offer much in the way of salary or benefits, it probably is not necessary for you to spend more money to advertise in the larger newspaper. Depending on the nature of the job, you might need to pick an international paper, such as the International Daily Herald, which is read world-wide. Generally, however, jobs of that nature are filled by using a headhunter or high-end recruitment agency (see Chapter 4).

Daily/Weekly/Monthly Publication

In addition to considering the circulation and target audience of the publication, you need to factor in its frequency. Is your need so pressing that you cannot wait the few days for your ad to appear? If this is the case and you are against using employment agencies, then a daily publication has to be your choice. If your search is more leisurely and you can wait, then using a targeted publication that is published less frequently is for you.

Internet Alone

The Internet is the current major player in the search for both jobs and qualified applicants. Websites such as Monster.com–the largest in the business–and Hotjobs.com reach far beyond any newspaper. According to Topjobsites.com, a Website that ranks the top job Websites, Monster.com has over 800,000 jobs and 130,000 employers listed with associated sites in more than 20 countries around the world. Besides the obvious advantage of enormous reach, these Websites allow candidates to search job type, location or keyword. These features help the candidate find the jobs that they are qualified for and interested in, which should decrease the number of resumes that you receive. This may not hold true if you allow candidates to apply for jobs through the Internet. Since it is so easy to apply in this way, employers often find themselves on the receiving end of many resumes from candidates who possess few of the skills they are looking for. Wording your ad carefully is doubly important online because you are reaching so many people. Nonetheless, being able to reach large numbers of job seekers may be worth that risk.

There are also hundreds of sites targeted to specific industries and positions. There are sites for health care, engineering, publishing, executives, airlines, and attorneys to name a few. Newer Websites such as Mkt10.com, developed by Careerbuilder.com's founder, approach the job seeker-potential employer relationship in a totally different way. Much like an online dating service, Mkt10.com asks candidates specific questions and then matches them to potential employers.

As always, be sure to check out the site you select. It is simple for someone to set up a Website, and unscrupulous persons may inflate their circulation and success rates, or they may just take your money without providing any services.

Internet in Combination with Hard Copy Publications

If your budget allows, you can use a variety of methods to advertise your search. Careerbuilder is owned by a conglomeration of newspapers, and allows you to place your ad both on their Website and in a newspaper concurrently, often at a considerable savings over placing the ads separately.

Your own Website

Many companies advertise solely on their own Website. While the exposure is often far less than on a Website or in a newspaper, the applications generally are a better match for the skills and experience required. To apply, applicants must have found you when looking for a specific field or location. This should weed out many completely unqualified candidates. Of course, you can use multiple advertising methods at the same time to maximize your exposure.

Finding qualified employees is not easy. It is a process involving time, money, and often frustration. By following the tips outlined above, you should be able to adequately advertise your position and hire the best employee for your open position. Spending the time to craft your ad copy and place it wisely will be well worth it in the end.

The Resources

General job seeker Websites include *www.monster.com*, *www.careerbuilder. com*, and *www.hotjobs.com*. Jobs specific to the U.S. government are frequently posted at *www.jobsearch.com*. Other Websites specifically targeted to industries are *www.dice.com* (technology), *www.efinancialcareers.com* (finance and commerce), and *www.healthcaresource.com* (health care).

Online Recruitment

Going High-Tech to Find Candidates

In recent years, online recruitment has grown from being a novelty in the high-tech sector to become commonplace across the entire employment spectrum. Estimates today suggest that online recruitment is the hiring method of choice for most entry-level, management and supervisory jobs. While the Internet may accelerate the hiring process, face-to-face interaction remains critical to selling and engaging the candidate. The following tips are useful guidelines for recruiting candidates via the Internet.

Attracting Candidates

Online recruitment enables a company to capitalize on its industry reputation and make its presence known to a wider range of job seekers. A corporate Website is a great vehicle for providing information about the company, its culture and environment, and its employment opportunities.

Sorting Resumes

Online recruitment not only makes it easy for job seekers to apply for positions, but it also enables companies to easily sift through a large number of applications. Software is also available to facilitate the sorting process. The software scores completed online applications against a model to determine if any meet the position's minimum qualifications.

Screening software may not be cost-effective for smaller businesses, however. Manual screening is still useful, but keep in mind that you may have many applications to screen if you are viewed as an employer of choice in your industry.

Here are some tips for reaching applicants online:

1. Know the criteria for screening.

   Some online search engines allow you to sort by skillset and geographical location, and you can further refine your results by job requirements and applicants' zip codes. The more detailed your search, the more qualified applicants you will find.

   Online job boards are useful for both companies and prospective employees; companies post available job opportunities, and prospective employees post their resumes for greater visibility. These boards are searchable using key words such as industrial engineer, administrative assistant, or paralegal. A search will generate a list of open positions from companies or resumes of interested candidates.

   If you define your desired criteria in advance of your hiring cycle, the resume pool resulting from your search will be more targeted to the available position, which will in turn reduce unnecessary time and effort on your part.

2. Use the full range of Internet options.

   Post job listings on popular career Websites such as Monster.com, Hotjobs.com, and CareerBuilder.com. These sites are frequently a first stop for applicants who use key words to search for opportunities that interest them. There are also industry-specific career sites that target candidates for more specialized positions. By tracking your success with different Internet sites, you will learn which will be most helpful to you in future hiring cycles.

3. Make sorting easier.

   If you receive hundreds of e-mail messages containing resumes from interested applicants, responding to each e-mail would be a formidable task. Some e-mail software applications allow you to create rules to sort incoming e-mail. Well-tailored rules help to separate those applicants who are well qualified from those who are not. There are additional technologies to assist you in all phases of the recruitment process, including job description creation, candidate mining, response management, and final hiring.

4. Do not waste time; rapid response is best.

   Many recruiters may be reviewing the same applicant's credentials at the same time, so your best approach is a quick response. There is little time to engage in a lengthy review process. Competition for qualified applicants is fierce, especially for those positions that require uncommon skillsets. These individuals may post their resume one week and be gone the next. If you can efficiently identify good candidates, interview and screen them, and make offers quickly, you will get the top talent that you need, without having to accept those who are less qualified for the job.

5. Identify worthy candidates for future opportunities.

During the hiring process, be alert for applicants who may be unsuitable for the present open position, but who may be suitable for a possible future position. Respond positively to them, and indicate that you will keep their information on file in order to contact them when the need arises. If you establish positive relationships with these applicants, you may fill future positions more easily than if you had started from scratch. Engaging the interest of potential future hires can be as easy as including them on an e-mail distribution list and asking them to inform you of any updates to their resumes.

6. Brand your own Website.

Post open positions on your corporate Website and encourage interested parties to submit their resumes for consideration. Potential applicants can learn more about your company, determine their level of interest in what you have to offer, and explore whether their qualifications may be attractive to you.

Advantages of Online Recruitment include:

Cost:
Internet advertising is significantly less expensive than more traditional advertising methods–perhaps as much as 75 percent less.

Time:
Employer surveys suggest that online applications and screening have cut the length of the typical hiring cycle in half.

Administration:
Electronic information storage, whether in-house or online, reduces paper usage and the time and space required to file that information.

Disadvantages of Online Recruitment Include:

Volume:
One online job posting can generate a considerable number of resumes to review and sort.

Qualifications:
Many applicants may not fit the basic qualifications for a position, leading to possible unnecessary communications with unsuitable candidates.

Reach:
Not all candidates are comfortable distributing personal information on the Internet. This may leave you with a narrow talent pool if you rely solely on online recruitment. This may also disadvantage older applicants who are either unfamiliar with or uncomfortable with using this technology to search for jobs.

In summary, the Internet is a great tool for both job seekers and for those offering jobs. Take the time to build your brand in cyberspace, and you will reap the rewards of greater visibility and speed in filling open positions.

The Resources

The Websites of the Society for Human Resource Management at *www.shrm.com* and the Workforce Management Resource Center at *www.workforce.com* both contain a wealth of information related to online recruitment.

The textbook *Human Resource Management* by Robert L. Mathis and John H. Jackson is now in its 11th edition and covers the entire range of human resources topics. It is available at Amazon at *www.amazon.com* or Barnes and Noble at *www.bn.com*.

7

Attracting Candidates: Employment Branding

Strong Branding Attracts Candidates

Attracting good candidates for open positions is critical to the hiring process. Studies have shown that reducing the time to fill open positions actually improves an organization's financial success. It stands to reason that the longer a position remains open, the less that position can contribute to organizational productivity and business outcomes.

Making an organization attractive to potential applicants provides a more robust talent pool when openings occur. Being known as a great place to work allows an organization to fill jobs quickly with the best talent. Organizations that create a favorable employment brand draw more applicants to each open position, obtain a higher caliber of applicants, and reduce the time required to fill those positions.

A strong employment branding strategy provides:

- A common theme, so that current employees express similar views on their experiences with the company.
- Visibility for the organization and for its products or services.
- Encouragement to job seekers to apply for opportunities within the organization.
- Information about the company culture and environment, work practices, and career development.
- Reinforcement for current employees as to the quality of the workforce and the value of their contributions.

Building an employment brand strategy takes time and effort. It usually starts with using any and all product or service marketing opportunities to link employment benefits. Here are some steps for building your employment brand strategy.

1. Define your current employment brand.

   Know where you stand right now with your employees and in the marketplace. In order to build an effective employment brand, you need to know the strength of your present brand and how it relates to your current needs.

2. Identify successful branding strategies in other organizations.

   Recognize successful branding strategies. Look at other organizations and what they have achieved through their branding efforts. You can also learn from organizations whose branding efforts have failed. Know what you must do to make your branding project successful. Then develop a list of criteria that will give your organization a reputation as a great place to work.

3. Identify the target market (candidates) for your branding effort.

   What types of candidates would you like to attract: college graduates, experienced professionals, or both? What are their target profiles, and where will you find them? The answers to these questions will help you to determine the methods by which you should advertise your brand.

4. Know your competitors' branding strategies.

   Look at your product competitors as well as your employment competitors. What messages do they project? How do those messages complement or detract from those messages your organization projects?

5. Assess what your organization currently offers.

   Examine your management practices, benefits, and company culture. Identify what you do well and what you need to enhance. Know what the competition is doing and how what you have to offer compares with the competition. Identify those areas in which you have the edge. For example, a larger organization can focus on career advancement, while a smaller organization can focus on employees' individual accomplishments.

6. Create a talent forecast.

   Define your needs for talent over the next 2 to 3 years. What critical skills, experience, and capabilities will be required to handle your future business challenges?

7. Develop a branding plan to build awareness.

   Use the information you have gathered to build a detailed plan of action. This should include those messages you would like to convey to candidates regarding:

- company culture
- management style
- current workforce
- long term opportunities
- image as leader in industry or community
- employment image
- learning and growth
- quality products

8. Get internal buy-in to the plan.

Your branding strategy will not succeed if you do not ensure that your managers and employees agree to it. A strong employment brand is consistent both within and outside the organization.

9. Monitor your progress.

Once you have implemented your branding plan, track its success through surveys, focus groups, and exit interviews. Know how others view you as an employer, and know how their views are shaped by your plan.

Your corporate Website is an ideal place to begin implementing your branding plan. Interested parties frequently access company Websites to learn about products, services and potential job opportunities. Ready access to career information and job postings helps to attract both active and passive job applicants. A successful corporate Website increases potential applicant traffic, returns accurate statistics on visitors to the site, and facilitates communication with interested parties.

Many employers work closely with brand marketing to link job and career information with product, media advertisement and community events. By exposing the community to the entire package, you can build brand loyalty to your products and services, and enhance the desirability of your employment opportunities.

Never underestimate your current employees. Word-of-mouth advertising is often useful in attracting new talent. Make it easy for them to refer job seekers to your organization. Referral programs offer a financial incentive for employees who refer job applicants who are subsequently hired. This incentive is a positive reinforcement for employees to continue their recruiting efforts. In the long run, an employee referral program costs less than many other recruitment methods, and it helps to enhance your organization's image as a great place to work.

The Resources

The Website *www.drjohnsullivan.com* as several articles on employment branding as well as additional links to related information.

8

Networking

How to Find Qualified Employees Everywhere

Most people think of networking only as a method for those looking for employment, but networking can be an effective method for employers trying to fill a difficult position. Employers are always looking for talent and trying new ways to find qualified candidates. Networking is also useful when you do not have an immediate need to employees, but would like to look toward the future.

Employers begin their search by listing all the possible sources for employment. Networking should be one of the first steps you take to find employees. It is not only a great way to learn about talented people, but it usually involves no costs.

How do you begin? First, consider all your potential sources or connections for your ideal employee. Examples of places to start include:

- Current employees
- Career and job fairs
- Colleagues in the same or similar businesses
- Customers and vendors
- Chambers of commerce and other business/service associations
- Nearby colleges and universities
- Friends, relatives, neighbors and other acquaintances

Current Employees

Believe it or not, your current employees are terrific resources and can be your best assets. Many companies pay referral fees to employees who find qualified employees that are hired for this very reason. Your current employees can be and often are your best source of advertising. Encourage your employees to tell their friends and families to consider working at your company. Your employees know the business and the pros and the cons of working there. They are familiar with your benefit package and any other perks you offer, and they know the company culture. Referral fees, even those of a few hundred dollars, are powerful incentives.

Career and Job Fairs

Career fairs and job fairs are large-scale events geared toward candidates from a particular field or geographical area. Many colleges and universities hold career fairs for their students, and in most instances, these fairs are also open to the public. The organizers will solicit area companies and encourage them to have a presence at the fair. Fairs targeted to job seekers in a particular field, such as health care or teaching, are an excellent way for you to build your base of candidates. You can collect resumes, e-mail addresses, and phone numbers for a large number of potential employees, usually for a single entry fee. You should consider participating in these fairs especially if you have immediate vacancies, but you can attend even if you have no positions currently available. Attrition is commonplace, and it is best to be prepared by having resumes and contact information for qualified candidates on hand.

Colleagues in the Same or Similar Business

You might think that your industry colleagues, being your competitors, would be unwilling to help you; this is typically not the case. Many industries have their own trade organizations where they meet regularly to share information. This information generally relates to a common problem or need, and employment issues are often a topic of discussion. Sometimes a company must reduce its workforce, or they may interview a candidate who does not fit its needs but who may be a valuable employee elsewhere. Although competing companies can have good working relationships, be advised that unscrupulous companies may try to steal away your star salesman or best employee.

Customers and Vendors

Do not overlook your customers and vendors. They know your company and your industry, and can probably point qualified individuals in your direction. Remember to be discreet, however, because your customers and vendors may also do business with your competitors.

Chambers of Commerce and Other Business/Service Associations

Most municipalities have chambers of commerce and service associations such as Rotary and Lions Clubs; all can be excellent sources of employment referrals. People who attend meetings and functions of these groups will undoubtedly know people that would be a wonderful match for your open positions. As an extra bonus, by participating in these organizations, you also spread goodwill about your company.

Nearby Colleges and Universities

List your openings at any colleges and universities that are near you. Depending upon the type of help you need, you may choose to include trade and vocational schools. Most high schools have a career contact person or department that works to place current students and alumni in appropriate jobs. This method can be an excellent way to locate a qualified employee that you would not have found by other methods.

Friends, Relatives, Neighbors and Other Acquaintances

Employment leads can come from anywhere. Sometimes your neighbor's first cousin's best friend's wife has the skills and knowledge you need to fill that difficult position. However, as with other search methods, you will never know that unless you advertise. Talking to people from all segments of your life is a sure-fire way to get your employment needs out there. It can be as simple as a casual mention at a party, a restaurant, or at the park. You can also raise the subject with church members, fellow school board members, or community volunteers. Your company has much to offer, and everyone knows someone who is either unemployed or interested in changing jobs. Most people want to help others; if they can help a friend or acquaintance find gainful employment and help you find a valuable employee, everyone wins.

Networking, like its counterparts employment agencies and classified ads, does not work all the time. It does, however, work most of the time. There is truth in the adage—It's not what you know, but who you know. People frequently land jobs for which they are perfectly qualified only because they knew someone with connections.

Networking is only one of the many resources you have when looking for good personnel. The wisest course is to use several methods to cover all the bases.

The Resources

Making a list of your current contacts is the best way to begin. Helpful Websites for chambers of commerce and other information include *www.uschamber.com*, *www.allbusiness.com* and *www.careerfairs.com*.

9

How to
Screen a Resume

Screen for the Best Candidates

No matter how you search for qualified candidates, whether through print advertisements, referrals, or Internet postings, you will be deluged with resumes from applicants with varied expertise–including many barely qualified for the position as advertised. At any given time, thousands of people are actively seeking new or better employment opportunities. From their perspective, they have nothing to lose and everything to gain in sending a resume and cover letter adapted to your specific job opening.

You, on the other hand, have many other responsibilities requiring your immediate attention. Although you are pressed for time, you need to hire a qualified individual who promises to be a long-term, productive employee. Above all, you want to avoid rehiring for the same position every 18 months. The hiring process is expensive and time consuming, and morale and productivity suffer when a position cannot be filled for any length of time.

If you intend to hire for several positions over time, you need to develop an efficient system to extract the resumes of qualified individuals from the deluge you receive. This system should focus on clearly defined goals and objectives, and a detailed job description for the position for which you are hiring.

Managers and business owners often wait for a crisis to occur before realizing there is more work than their employees can handle. They react by hastily posting an advertisement in the paper or on the Internet, without a clear understanding of the company's real needs. The better approach is to take the long view, assemble your team or key managers, and determine your goals and objectives for the next 12 to 18 months. Your plan should be flexible to allow for unexpected personnel changes, business volume or shifting department priorities. If you have clearly defined your goals and objectives, you will better understand why you are hiring and who is your ideal candidate–at least on paper.

You should also take the time to write a detailed job description. Determine a salary range that is in line with current employees in similar positions. Clearly indicate who will train and manage the new employee. An accurate job description allows you to objectively evaluate applicants and determine the best candidates for the position.

Ideally, a resume details an individual's professional experience and educational background. Evidence suggests, however, that one-third to one-half of all job applicants misrepresent themselves on their resumes. Therefore, it is critical to screen all resumes. When you interview a candidate, verify the information on his or her resume. After the interview, check the candidates references.

Remember that screening is only the first step in the hiring process; it is an attempt to separate the reasonably qualified from those who are not at all qualified for your advertised position.

Tips for Screening Resumes

You can quickly screen a large number of resumes by focusing on these key areas:

Look at the overall layout.
> Does the resume give a good first impression? Are the applicant's credentials clearly organized and concise?

Check the job summary.
> Is it aligned with the position that you need to fill? You want to interview those applicants who are genuinely interested in this position.

Review responsibilities.
> Does the applicant have the experience required for the position? Is there a pattern of increased responsibility? Is the applicant overqualified for this position?

Check dates of employment.
> Are they consistent with the job application? Identify any breaks in service or other irregularities.

Observe grammar and punctuation.
> A resume usually reflects an individual's best communications skills. Mistakes of this kind on a resume may foreshadow errors in their on-the-job work.

Focus on results.
> What did the applicant achieve on previous work assignments? Place less emphasis on tasks or activities.

Evaluate education or training.

Does the applicant have the requisite level of education or training? Is the information credibly identified?

Note special skills.

Has the applicant listed any skills that may enhance his or her ability to perform in this position?

Assume that you screened 10 resumes from a pool of more than 40 applicants. Each of the 10 resumes matches your objectives and job description in one way or another. Now you should rank them according to how well they match your requirements. Circulate resumes among other managers and team members, who should also rank them in the same manner. Once everyone has ranked the resumes, you may be able to reduce the pool to three or four applicants. You can then devote additional time to further screening, background checks, interviews, and employment verification.

Remember to treat a resume like an application. Even if an applicant supplies information that the employer is not legally allowed to request (e.g., regarding age, religion, or marital status), that information must be ignored during the entire hiring process.

It is always a good idea to ask candidates to complete an employment application. You may find contradictions when you cross-check facts between the application and the resume. The application should require the applicant's signature, with a statement certifying that all information they have provided is correct. The application should also identify what consequences will result (e.g., termination of employment) if any statements are found to be untrue. This policy may well deter those applicants who may have exaggerated on their resumes.

Employers are not required to retain the records of applicants who are not considered for the position. Resumes that have been screened and that fit the basic criteria for the position should be kept on file for 2 years, even if that applicant is not hired.

In summary, employers must be:

- Be clear about the specifics of the job before screening resumes.
- Be consistent and develop written protocols for screening resumes.
- Train those who review resumes to use the protocol you have developed.
- Check periodically to ensure that those who review resumes comply with the screening protocol and 2-year data retention policy.

The Resources

The Website of the U.S. Department of Labor at *www.dol.gov* contains a vast amount of general information concerning hiring and employment law. Among the many features of this site–all of which are free–is the Employer Assistance and Recruiting Network (EARN), which is designed to place qualified individuals with disabilities.

10

Telephone Screening

Getting Organized

Employers frequently prescreen candidates with a telephone interview before scheduling an onsite interview, especially when out-of-town travel is required or when candidates are employed elsewhere. A telephone screen should follow a prescribed protocol similar to that of the resume screen. A typical telephone screen might include the following:

- Explain the purpose of your call. Identify yourself, state that you have received their resume or application, and that you would like to schedule an initial telephone discussion. Explain that the call would last about 15 minutes.

- Clarify an acceptable time for the telephone discussion. Ask whether the applicant has time to talk now, or whether a mutually acceptable time is more appropriate. The applicant may choose to proceed right away–knowing that the call should only last about 15 minutes–or may choose to prepare for a discussion at a later date.

- Ask the applicant five to 10 screening questions. You should have identified a number of items during the resume screen that will determine whether the applicant will make the cut. Such items might include the candidate's continued interest in the position and company; compensation; relocation; willingness to travel; availability for shift work; and previous experiences that match present needs.

- Determine whether to progress further with the candidate. Use their answers to the above questions to determine if they fit the basic criteria and should continue in the interview process. You also want to determine their level of interest in further discussions and interviews.

- If you feel that the candidate should not continue in the process, you can either inform them that they do not fit the criteria, or let them know that you will inform them in writing as to their continued candidacy. If you feel that the candidate fits the criteria and has a continued interest in the position, you can explain the next steps in the interviewing process. Such steps may include onsite interviews, additional telephone interviews, or a battery of tests designed to assess the applicant's skills.

An interview screen saves time, both for the candidate and for the employer. In 15 minutes, you should be able to establish a candidate's viability for the position and arrange a follow-up interview

---

You can adapt the following sample telephone screen protocol to meet your needs.

Sample Telephone Pre-Interview Screen Document

Date: _____ Position applied for: _____

Candidate Name: _____

Phone Work: _____ Home: _____

1. Identify self, company, and position. Indicate why you are calling.

2. Give brief description of the position. Be sure to present both positives and negatives.

3. Ask prepared questions

   • Are you currently available?   Yes ___   No ___

If no, when?

   • Notice period required?
   • Verify employment background.
   • Availability to travel.
            Yes ___ No ___ If yes, to what extent (_____%)?
   • Are you open to relocation? If yes, desired areas?
   • What shifts can you work?
   • Can you work weekends?
   • Current rate of pay?
      – the compensation (describe):
   • Pay requirements:
   • Reason for seeking new position:

Interviewer evaluation:

Yes___ (Tell the applicant what will happen next, i.e. time and place for interview.)

No___ (Thank the applicant for the time and indicate that after review of all applicants you will be in touch if there is further interest.)

More on Telephone Screening

In order to be truly effective with the telephone screening process, you need to be able to make a go or no-go decision while the candidate is still on the phone. (This assumes, of course, that you do not need to call the candidate back because they are not able to speak at length.)

Assuming the individual has demonstrated that he has potential, close the conversation with a firm commitment to meet the candidate personally. After arranging a time to meet, explain who will be interviewing the candidate and what the overall timetable for a decision is. The point is to save time; why call back if you know you want this individual to come in for an interview?

Make sure that you get an e-mail address in case you need to send additional information. Also, allow the candidate to ask questions. You may find that the questions will short-cut the process even more.

The Resources

For more information on telephone screening, visit *www.shrm.com*.

The Hiring Source Book, Catherine D. Fyock will offer more detail on this and related subjects.

11

Resume Storage & Retrieval

Determining If and When You Should Hold an Application

In a perfect world, after advertising for an open position you will easily select the most qualified candidate from a list of hopefuls. You make the job offer, he or she accepts, you come to terms regarding salary and benefits, and you have a new employee. Most of the time, however, you will have a list of several candidates who could be terrific employees.

How do you store this valuable information? The answer might depend upon what format the information is in. You may need a paper filing system, because some candidates mail or fax their resumes and cover letters. Many hiring professionals prefer paper submissions because they are easier to read and organize. If you have many paper resumes and applications for which you have no immediate need, you must determine whether to keep them. Your decision should be based upon the following criteria:

- Do you have the physical space to retain these documents?
- Do you want to keep them? Some or all?
- When do you anticipate having an opening for a similar position?
- Are these candidates qualified for other positions?

No one wants to pay for space they do not need. The widespread use of computers has enabled companies to reduce their filing space; as a result, there is often little space left in which to file employment-related information. If this situation applies to you, then the answer to the question is simple: You cannot keep the documents.

If you have the space, but lack the means to handle this information, you can either toss it or organize your space. This scenario requires you to first consider whether you are interested in retaining the documents. If the answer is yes, then you need to designate an area just for resumes and applications from previous job candidates.

Once you decide that you are interested in keeping the information, you then need to figure out how to arrange the information. Filing cabinets do not take up much room and truly lend themselves to organization. If you choose to keep the documents in a file cabinet, you must devise a system for quickly finding information when you need it. You can organize the resumes and applications by position, alphabetically by applicant's last name, by date, or by any other method that seems logical to you. Most importantly, it must be a system that you are comfortable following and that will be easy to maintain.

Your purpose in keeping these documents should be clear before you choose a filing method. Are you keeping the information because you know you are experiencing a great deal of turnover in a particular position or department? If this is the case, then you might want to file the resumes by department so you will know which ones to turn to should another vacancy arise. The danger in this method is the possibility of typecasting certain candidates. Perhaps you feel the candidate would be perfect for marketing or sales. Should you file this candidate under sales or marketing? If a sales position becomes vacant, but this candidate is filed under marketing, you may completely forget about this candidate. In this instance, the time and effort spent in retaining this information will be wasted.

Did you really like a particular candidate after the interview, but later realize he or she might fit into several positions? In this circumstance, you may consider filing the information alphabetically by applicant's name. A good tip is to place a large sticky note on the front of the resume or application that lists a few of the candidate's strengths. This way, when you look through your filing system for viable candidates, you can pull the ones that have the skills or experience you seek.

A system that is organized by date of last contact with the candidate is easy to keep current. You decide how long you want to keep a resume, and periodically toss those that become stale. There is no need to sift through every one to see if it has become dated; your system will let you know.

It is important to gauge how long you intend to keep resumes and applications on file–6 months, a year, or even just a month. It is also important to know why you intend to keep the information. If you know that you will need to fill additional positions in the same department in another month or so, then it makes sense to keep the information on your applicant pool. You can save valuable time and money if much of your work is done ahead of time. On the other hand, if you know that you will not need the information within a short period of time, then you need not waste valuable office space on that information.

If the applications and resumes are electronic, whether to keep them will not be based upon physical space but on other criteria. If you are convinced that the information will be helpful to you, then by all means develop an electronic filing system for storing the information and preserving the data. Any of the systems described for paper resumes work well for electronic files. An advantage of electronic storage is the ability to find information quickly no matter how it is organized. You can search your computer for names, skills, areas of expertise, and positions desired in a few seconds. This will undoubtedly save you quite a bit of time.

Although it is easy to keep applications and resumes on file, many companies and organizations simply do not. There are many reasons for this. First, they have discovered that when they contact an applicant even a month later, the applicant is no longer interested or has another job. Second, applicants can move or change their contact information, making interaction impossible. Third, it may seem easier to conduct a search for each position rather than take the time to search through archived information.

Whether you opt to keep the applications and resumes on file or get rid of them once the position is filled, it is common courtesy to inform the candidates of your policy if they ask. Your philosophy may be to file old information by position only; if that is the case, you need to inform the candidates that they will have to apply again if they find another position that they are interested in. Whether you keep applications and resumes on file or toss, the candidates should know whether they will have to apply again or if you will contact them if they are a good match.

The Resources

Large companies are often challenged by records management, storage and retrieval. Companies such as Xerox provide assistance and solutions. Visit *www.xerox.com* for more information.

Websites such as *www.filetrail.com* advertise software solutions to record management and retrieval. This is just one of many available vendors.

12

The Interview

Conducting a Legal, Productive Interview

After you have determined your vacancy, written your job description, advertised your position, screened the resumes you received, and selected the candidates you are interested in, the fun really begins. You now need to schedule appointments to interview the candidates and find the one you want to hire.

Before you can even contemplate actually conducting interviews, you need to prepare carefully. Things to consider before you actually begin interviewing should include:

- Will the employee fill out an application before the interview? If you do not have a company application, consider purchasing one from the Internet or any bookstore. Ensure that the application does not contain any illegal questions (see below and Chapter 13).
- Who will do the interviewing?
- Will human resources do the preliminary screening?
- Will the department's manager or supervisor handle the task?
- Will potential team members meet or interview the applicant?
- Where will the interview take place?
- Will the interview be in multiple stages or is one sufficient?
- What kind of interview will it be? Some types of interviews include:
    - Traditional
    - Behavioral
    - Group
    - Committee
    - Audition
    - Stress

Traditional Interviews

Traditional interviews are the most straightforward, but they do not necessarily focus only on a candidate's skills and experience. Presumably, your earlier selection process would have weeded out unqualified applicants and left you only with those that have the proper qualifications. Now you need to see how well he or she will fit into your company and what type of employee he or she will make. Questions typically asked in a traditional interview include:

- How would you describe yourself?
- Where do you see yourself in the next 5 years?
- Why did you leave your last job?
- What are your short- and long-range goals?
- How do you handle pressure?
- Why did you seek a position in this particular company?

Behavioral Interviews

Behavioral interviews were developed to see how candidates handle certain situations. They focus on how a job seeker reacts to problems and common business scenarios. You should use a range of situations both with positive and negative perspectives so you see how the candidate reacts in each type of circumstance. Questions that you would use in a behavioral interview include:

- Give me an example of a difficult decision you had to make.
- Tell me about a time when you had too many tasks and had to prioritize your work. What method did you employ? Was it successful?
- How do you handle conflict? Have you ever had to work with a peer or supervisor that you did not like? How did you work around that?
- Give me an example of how you motivate others.
- Tell me about a time when you missed a deadline or set a goal and were unable to meet it.
- Describe a time when you anticipated problems and developed a proactive solution.

Group Interviews

Group interviews, in which top candidates are interviewed concurrently, are often conducted during the second phase of interviewing. They are most often used to discover leadership and management potential in high-end candidates. Rather than ask pointed questions to one candidate at a time, you begin a discussion and see how each candidate interacts with the others. Using questions commonly used in behavioral interviews will be the most successful in a group interview, because they provide an excellent springboard for discussion and allow you to get to the heart of the matter. You can also evaluate body language and interpersonal skills much better in a group setting than in a one-on-one interview. Remember to take copious notes so that you can keep track of and compare the candidates.

Committee Interviews

Committee interviews enable multiple people in your organization to meet the candidate at one time. This type of interview is used most often in companies that emphasize team cooperation. A group interview allows current employees to interact with the candidate and determine whether he or she is a good fit for the team. Traditional and behavioral questions are appropriate in this type of interview.

Audition Interviews

Audition interviews require candidates to perform specific tasks, and enable employers to see a potential employee in action. You might ask the candidate to solve a computer problem if you are looking for computer technicians, or set up mock customer service calls to see how he or she handles telephone communication. Typing or business writing tests are forms of audition interviews that are incorporated into behavioral and traditional interviews.

Most one-on-one interviews are combinations of both traditional and behavioral interviews with components of the audition interview thrown in. By combining your approaches, you will come away with a well-developed image of your candidates.

Stress Interviews

Stress interviews are designed to make a candidate uncomfortable and often do more harm than good. Two techniques often used in this type of interview are not making eye contact during the interview and keeping a candidate waiting for more than a few minutes. If you want to get the most from your candidate during the interview, avoid these techniques, which appear boorish to some and can get you into legal trouble. It is for this reason that stress interviews are relatively uncommon.

Once you have decided what kind or kinds of interview styles you are going to use and the logistics are taken care of, you need to decide what questions you are going to ask. The importance of planning what you are going to ask and knowing what you cannot ask cannot be overemphasized. If other employees will participate in the interview, make sure that they are well trained in the questions they should ask. Forgetting to ask a critical question may lead you to hire someone completely wrong for the position. Asking the wrong questions can make you a defendant in an expensive lawsuit. Having a set of prepared questions will help you avert both bad decisions and disasters.

As discussed more thoroughly in Chapter 13, questions about the following topics are illegal and cannot be asked under any circumstances:

- age
- arrests
- birthplace
- color
- disability
- marital/family status
- national origin
- personal
- race
- religion
- sex

While it is important to know what you cannot ask, you need to know what you can ask and what you should ask. A great deal of information about your candidate will be available both from the resume and from the application that was filled out. This information primarily consists of basic information such as name, address, phone number, education and previous work experience. Skills and interests are also typically available on a resume or on an application. You need to use the interview to get past the basic, run-of-the mill information and get to the heart of your candidate. After all, this is not any ordinary candidate; this is a potential new employee for your company.

The Resources

Various Internet sites provide a wealth of information on conducting interviews, including *www.allbusiness.com*, *www.monster.com*, and *www.interview-questions.org*. Many of these sites approach the topic from the candidate's point of view, but it is simple to turn the information around to help you conduct a fair and productive interview.

You can also consult the Websites of the Equal Employment Opportunity Commission (*www.eeoc.gov*) and the Department of Labor (*www.dol.gov/dol/topic/discrimination*) for information on federal discrimination laws. Chapter 1 of this book also provides a primer on those employment laws with which you should be familiar.

13
Questions You Should Not Ask When Hiring

The Problems That Can Occur

It is illegal for potential employers to ask certain questions of job applicants at any stage in the hiring process. Some questions may not be asked, no matter how casual, how informal, or how innocuous they may seem to you. For example, if you even hint that you would like to know a candidate's age, you may quickly find yourself not only without a candidate but also in serious legal trouble. While there is a difference between questions that are inappropriate and those that are illegal, both are to be avoided. Questions to avoid fall under the following categories:

- age
- arrests
- birthplace
- color
- disability
- marital/family status
- national origin
- personal
- race
- religion
- sex

These categories are based upon federal discrimination laws which are enforced by the Equal Employment Opportunity Commission (EEOC) and may differ from your state laws. The federal laws are typically the minimum standards that a company must follow; state laws are often stricter. Familiarizing yourself with federal, state and local laws and statutes is crucial to conducting fair and legal interviews. Some of these laws include:

- Title VII of the Civil Rights Act of 1964.
- The Age Discrimination in Employment Act.
- The Equal Pay Act.

- The Immigration Reform and Control Act.
- The Americans with Disabilities Act.

Most inappropriate questions are asked out of ignorance, usually by those new to hiring or employees in companies without a formal human resources department. These questions are often asked simply to make the candidate feel at ease and to take some of the tension out of the interview. During an interview, you need to learn a great deal of information about a candidate in a short period of time. Those well-intentioned sentiments and those concerns lead you to ask those questions you simply cannot ask.

The EEOC has documented that most incidents of discrimination occur during the hiring process. Since the interview is one of the key components of this process, it is imperative that all personnel involved in the interview know and understand the rules. The object of these laws is to ensure that all applicants receive equal employment opportunity.

There may often be times when you may legally obtain some of these answers, however. In a few instances, appropriate questions may be asked to discover sensitive information. The applicant may have volunteered such information in a resume or references, or may unexpectedly reveal information in answers to legitimate interview questions.

You can ensure compliance with the law by writing your questions down and sticking to them. Have them in front of you during the interview so you will stay on track. Another important rule is to ask the same questions of all applicants to ensure that you follow EEOC procedures by leveling the playing field. If you are unsure whether a certain question is appropriate, ask yourself whether it is a legitimate bona fide occupational qualification (BFOQ).

What You Should Not Ask

The following are examples of both inappropriate and appropriate ways to elicit information from a job applicant.

Subject Area: Age	
Inappropriate:	How old are you? When were you born? When did you graduate high school?
Appropriate:	Are you over the age of 18?

Subject Area: Birthplace/national origin

Inappropriate:	Where were you born? How long have you lived in the United States? Where were your parents from? What language do you speak at home?
Appropriate:	Are you authorized to work in the United States?

The temptation here might be to ask whether the applicant is fluent languages other than English. This question is only appropriate if the position requires multilingual skills.

Subject Area: Personal

Inappropriate:	How tall are you? How much do you weigh?
Appropriate:	Can you lift and carry a 40-pound box of books 150 yards?

Again, this should only be asked if it is a BFOQ.

Subject Area: Disability

Inappropriate:	Do you have any use of your legs? How long have you been in the wheelchair? What is your medical history?
Appropriate:	List the physical requirements needed to perform tasks of the job (e.g., heavy lifting) and ask whether the applicant is able to perform those tasks.

Subject Area: Marital/family status

Inappropriate:	Are you married? Do you have any children? Do you plan on having any children? What are your child care arrangements?
Appropriate:	Are you willing to relocate? Are you able to travel?

These questions are appropriate as long as they are asked of all applicants.

You may be able to infer a candidate's information by carefully checking his or her resume and references. For instance, while you cannot ask about a candidate's religious preference, his or her resume may list membership in a church, synagogue, other religious organization. Other information may include political and social affiliations and trade and professional organizations.

Some companies use personality or psychometric tests as additional screening tools. At first glance, these appear to be beneficial, especially if the tests come from a legitimate source. The problem is that many of these tests, even published ones, may contain illegal or inappropriate questions and should therefore be avoided. Even those tests developed by reputable companies have also come under extra scrutiny in recent years. In June of 2005, the Seventh Circuit held that the Minnesota Multi-Phasic Personality Inventory (MMPI) was a medical examination under the Americans with Disabilities Act. The court stated that the use of this test during the hiring process is illegal, because the test questions discriminate against job applicants with disabilities. Standard business-skills tests that measure typing ability, computer expertise, business writing proficiency and the like are perfectly acceptable, however.

An effective interviewer asks pertinent, appropriate questions to determine whether an applicant will be a good fit for the open position. Discovering a person's relevant job qualifications requires perseverance, knowledge of the law, and the ability to synthesize information obtained from various sources. Spending the time to make sure that you ask the right questions will pay off every time.

The Resources

Visit the Website of the Equal Employment Opportunity Commission at *www.eeoc.gov* for a wealth of information regarding federal EEO laws, discriminatory practices, and compliance information.

The U.S. Department of Labor has a Webpage devoted specifically to discrimination, *www.dol.gov/dol/topic/discrimination*. Critical topics include compliance assistance, state labor offices, and an extensive research library.

Findlaw's small-business section *http://smallbusiness.findlaw.com/employment-employer/employment-employer-discrimination/employment-employer-discrimination-laws-federal.html* covers many issues unique to small businesses face and presents its material in a concise, easy-to-read format.

14

Employment Verification

Checking Out the Facts

Background checks on prospective hires are strongly recommended to help employers avoid hiring an individual with a questionable personal or professional background. The background check usually takes place after the interviewer decides that the applicant is qualified and is a good fit for the available position.

The Fair Credit Reporting Act (FCRA) states how background checks may be conducted, how the information thus obtained may be used, and the rights of the individual whose background is under investigation. There are four steps an employer must take to ensure basic compliance with the FCRA:

Step 1. Disclosure and Written Authorization.

The employer must give the job applicant a special notice in writing that the employer will request an investigative report. The applicant must give signed consent to the investigation. The employer must also provide the applicant with a summary of their rights under federal law. The applicant may request a copy of the investigative report.

Step 2. Certification to the Federal Consumer Reporting Agency (FCRA).

Before an employer may obtain an investigative consumer report, it must provide proper certification to the applicable consumer reporting agency. Most agencies require employers to sign a certification agreement. The agreement stipulates that, by signing, the employer agrees to comply with the FCRA in all of its interactions with the job applicant.

Step 3. Providing Copies of Reports and Waiting a Reasonable Time Before Taking Adverse Action.

A copy of the report must be given to the job applicant, who must have a reasonable amount of time in which to dispute the wrongful use or interpretation of the information, and to request corrections where necessary.

Step 4. Notice After Adverse Action.

An employer may take adverse action (e.g., by removing an applicant from further consideration) if the investigation reveals disqualifying information. The employer need not explain the nature of the adverse action to the job applicant.

Work Reference Checking

Always obtain an applicant's permission in writing to verify employment history and conduct a background check. Note that previous employers are often reluctant to provide information about their former employees, even when the candidate has given permission for the release of such information. Most companies will only verify dates of employment, job title, and perhaps the salary of a former employee. Generally, companies do not comment on one's qualifications, job performance or reason for departure.

Companies often check a candidate's academic credentials, credit history (if pertinent to the position), motor vehicle record, and criminal background record.

It is advisable to ask candidates under consideration to provide references, preferably from former supervisors. If you can establish a professional rapport with a candidate's former supervisor, you can often obtain valuable and pertinent information as to the candidate's past work performance, work habits, attitude, and accomplishments. References may also expound upon information a candidate has supplied on an application or resume. Always be well prepared when talking with references. Have your questions outlined in advance so that you may legally cover the information needed to make a sound hiring decision. Consider the discussion an interview: ask open-ended questions when possible, and probe for the information you need. It is best to start with factual questions before moving to those involving a candidate's work habits and style. Areas to explore should include:

- Technical or functional skills and abilities
- Work style and standards
- Personal initiative
- Maturity and professionalism
- Culture fit

The following sample reference check is a guide for your use:

Reference Check Guide

Introduction:

Hello, my name is _____ from _____ [organization]. Thank you for agreeing to give me a few minutes to talk about [candidate's name] and [his/her] candidacy for the position [name of position] in our organization. I'm hoping to get your insights on [his/her] strengths, possible areas for development, and work styles.

Let's start with how long have you [known/worked] with _____?

What was/is the working relationship?

   Boss

   Colleague

   Subordinate

What do you believe are [his/her] greatest strengths?

Based upon the position outlined, what do you believe are one or two areas I should focus on for development?

Would you rate the following attributes on a high, moderate or low scale, and possibly give me an example?

Criteria	Rating			Example
Technical/Functional Job Skills	H	M	L	
Work Style & Standards Punctual Work ethic Quality output	H	M	L	
Personal Initiative Self starter Multi-tasking	H	M	L	
Maturity & Professionalism Judgment Decision Making	H	M	L	
Culture Fit Team Player Social	H	M	L	
Other	H	M	L	

Do you have any additional advice on ways to best manage [him/her] in this position?

Thank you so much for your time and helpful comments.

In summary, never hire an employee without checking references, since unfortunately, many candidates feel the need to embellish their achievements and credentials.

The Resources

You can download a copy of the Reference Check Guide from Encouragement Press *www.encouragementpress.com*.

Further information about fair credit reporting and related issues can be found at the Federal Trade Commission's Website, *www.ftc.gov/credit*, along with a downloadable version of *A Summary of Your Rights Under The Fair Credit Reporting Act*.

15

Selection of Candidate/ Extending the Offer

Selecting the Best Candidate and Making the Offer

The moment has finally arrived. You have successfully interviewed your candidates using the processes outlined in Chapter 12 and you are ready to make your selection. Unless one candidate has stood out among the rest and you have a clear choice, you will need to evaluate all the information you have gathered in order to make the best decision. This decision often gets put off due to workload or other concerns, but it should really be handled in a timely manner. If you wait too long to decide on a new hire, you run the risk that he or she will no longer be available. It is important to make the time to find a good quality employee that you want to hire.

Steps to Follow When Evaluating Applicants

1. Decide whether the decision will be made by an individual or by committee.

   a. If you are going to make this decision primarily on your own, clear an hour or two from your calendar, close your door, and let all calls go to voicemail.
   b. Check to make sure you have feedback from others in your company who may have spoken with the applicant.
   c. If the decision is to be made by committee, find a time to meet and stick to it. Make sure that you allot enough time to review each candidate.

2. Inform others not involved in the hiring process that you are not to be disturbed. Because this work does not have an impact on current day-to-day operations, others may assume that what you are doing is not that crucial and that you are interruptible. In fact, the opposite is true. Constant disruptions are distracting and can cause you to act in haste just so you can finish and get back to your other work. Allowing the proper amount of undisturbed time will contribute greatly to your success in hiring the right candidate.

3. Gather the resumes, applications and any other information you have pertaining to the top candidates.

4. Clear your desk (or the conference table if you are doing this in a group) and begin reviewing the candidates.

5. Clarify what you are looking for in a candidate.

   a. List qualities, skills and experience the candidate must have.
   b. List qualities, skills and experience you would like the candidate to have.
   c. List qualities, skills and experience that would be beneficial in the job, but not necessary.
   d. Reread the job description you created for the position.

6. Reread each resume generally to refresh your mind and help you to remember each particular candidate. Go over the candidate's application carefully and double check the notes that were taken on each candidate. If you did not take the notes and discover that something is unclear, do not assume that it is unimportant and ignore it. Find the author of the notes, if he or she is not in the room with you, and ask them to elaborate.

7. Check each resume thoroughly for unexplained gaps. Also check the application and notes against the resume and against each other to make sure that there are no contradictions.

8. Look for errors or inconsistencies in the resume. Nearly half of all job applicants manipulate facts on their resume. Some people excel in creating previous positions for themselves or inventing degrees from schools that they never attended. Be vigilant so you do not get stung. Hiring someone that is ultimately found to have misrepresented their credentials can cost the company significant time, effort, money and reputation.

9. Place a large sticky note on each candidate's packet. Write several one- or two-word descriptions of each candidate that highlight his or her strengths and weaknesses.

10. Review your data and rank the candidates. If you are deciding this as a collective effort, it is likely that the candidates will be ranked differently by each decision-maker. You then need to discuss each candidate. Each person involved in the hiring decision should explain his or her ranking and the reasons behind them.

11. Select your new hire.

   While it may seem that you are all set to make the call, you need to do one thing more before you take the plunge. You must conduct a background check on your candidate so that you do not later regret your hiring decision. A background check must be done in any hiring situation.

First, contact all of the candidate's references. Do not stop at the first one or overlook them completely. Contacting references is sound business practice. Many companies are reluctant to give out negative information about a former employee out of fear of being sued. If possible, you should have potential hires sign a waiver authorizing you to contact their former employers to ask detailed questions.

When you contact the candidate's previous employers, fax a copy of the waiver to them so they will know that they can be truthful and share the information. Use this opportunity to also verify basic information about the candidate: date of hire, positions held, etc. Pay attention to any lukewarm or negative references. Most people try to find something good to say about others; if the reference can only come up with half-hearted words of praise, this may be a sign that you need to rethink your decision. Conversely, this candidate still may be a terrific employee and the reference may have personal reasons for their responses, so you need to be careful. This is another reason why you should perform due diligence and contact all the references given to you.

Check the person out on the Internet. Putting his or her name into a search engine such as Google or Yahoo can provide you with information that you would never had found anywhere else. Of course, not everything posted on the Internet is true, but it may tip you off that something is not right. Take the results of your search with a grain of salt.

When you are comfortable that the person you have chosen is the right person, you can get ready to make the phone call offering the candidate the opportunity to join your company. Items that you will want to cover in this conversation include:

- Position offered
- Salary
- Start date
- Hours of work week
- Benefits
  - Medical
  - Dental
  - Vision
  - Vacation
  - Sick or personal time
- Bonus (if any)
- Probationary period (if applicable)
- Eligibility of candidate to work in the United States

You will more fully explain these conditions of employment on your new hire's first day or at orientation, you should mention them during the offer phone call so the candidate can decide whether to accept your offer.

Do not be surprised if the candidate asks for some time to think about your offer. In some cases, you will get a response immediately, but many people require time to consider their options. You should also be prepared if the candidate begins to negotiate some aspect of the package. The negotiation is usually, but not always, about salary. The candidate might say that he or she was told a different number when he or she interviewed or that this salary just will not work. You also have the option of telling the candidate that you will get back to him or her, but you should certainly know what you are willing to offer on the spot.

Once the candidate has accepted, many companies follow up with an employment letter confirming salary and date of hire. This letter should also mention that the new hire will have employment at-will status, so that the letter is not considered a contract.

Now that you have selected your candidate and called to make your offer, the next step is out of your hands. If the candidate's answer is no, you can move to the second-ranked person on your list. If the answer is yes and all the terms are agreed upon, then you have a new employee.

The Resources

Websites that address selection of candidates and the offer process include *www.smartbiz.com*, *www.shrm.org* (Society for Human Resource Management), and *www.smallbizresource.com*.

16

Negotiation

The Art and Science

Negotiation is nothing more than coming to terms on a single matter or a range of issues. In either case, it is one of the great arts in business and it is an essential function when hiring and firing employees. If you have already determined your employment needs, written job descriptions, and created an employee manual, then it would seem that there is little to negotiate with prospective employees. In fact, there may be a great deal more to negotiate, and those items vary depending on the level of the job. Negotiating with a potential clerical employee is entirely different from negotiating with a senior executive.

This is a partial list of some common areas for negotiation when hiring:

- Salary and fringe benefits
- Stock options
- Travel requirements
- Bonuses and other incentives
- Vacation (assuming that you do not have a fixed policy for all employees)
- Starting date
- Job responsibilities
- Severance package
- Non-compete agreement
- Job title
- Direct reports
- Moving expenses and mortgage assistance
- Severance package in the event of involuntary termination

Consider some of the issues may have to be negotiated when an employee is fired:

- Severance
- References
- Use of an office

- Release of a non-compete agreement
- Company-paid insurance benefits

There are a couple of different strategies you can take when negotiating with future employees: hard-line negotiating and win-win negotiating.

Hard line negotiators are always careful to stack the cards to the company's benefit. But consider if such a strategy is really good for the employer/employee relationship over the long run. In theory you are hiring an employee for the long-term. Put yourself in the employee's shoes. If he or she walks away because there is no room for negotiation, then you have lost a potentially solid employee. Remember that if this person is already employed, even though they want to leave for whatever reasons, they still have a job and could easily decide that the negotiations on salary and other issues are a harbinger of the future.

Win-win negotiators give a little and take a little to reach an intended outcome. This strategy usually works best for both parties, and this approach has been emphasized in business literature for many years. It emphasizes the need for each party in the negotiations to feel that they have won something, perhaps an important concession from their point of view.

When negotiating with employees, do not focus just on the budget or the personal challenge of getting what you want. Rather, look behind the discussions and determine what you really need. You need a qualified individual who has the skills and background for the open position, and is also the right fit for your company's culture. It may cost a bit more and you may have to concede on some issues. Ask yourself whether the benefits are worth the risks.

Here are four helpful tips for successful negotiation:

1. Be prepared

    Take the time before a candidate comes to your office to know what you must have and what you can concede. Presumably the candidate has been interviewed previously, either by an associate, on the phone, or by a hiring specialist in your company. Speak to others who have met or have been involved with this candidate and try to understand what this individual feels is important.

2. Set the proper tone for the meeting

    Be friendly, professional and firm. Start with a leading question; allow the candidate to have the floor first. This will allow you to learn this individual's needs or wants.

3. Explore needs

> Set aside all other issues and focus on what the future employee needs. Once this is confirmed, other issues become minor. At no time is there a need to talk; the less you speak, the more you allow the individual to explain his or her needs.

4. Propose an offer

> Based on what you have learned and what you need to have as an employer, make an offer and ask for comments or reactions. Alternatively, you can recap the discussion and propose an offer at a later time. In either case, any offer is contingent on a background check and other standard operating procedures before formal employment begins.

Salary is certainly the most important point of negotiation for both parties and a salary discussion is often the most difficult and the most critical discussion you may have with an employee. You know your range, as you have pegged it already to a job description and to salaries to employees with similar jobs. On the other hand, you may be willing to extend the range somewhat in order to attract a particularly good candidate. When discussing salary, it is always a game of who goes first. You ask what the candidate's expectations are; the clever candidate will demure and try to get you to give an indication of your salary range. As a rule, you should not post salaries or salary ranges when advertising for a position. You may be able to hire a fine employee for thousands less than you thought and still have an individual who feels properly compensated.

Do not allow your impressions of a candidate–whether positive or negative–to cloud your understanding of the going rate for salary and other compensation. Know the industry and/or local standards for compensation. If necessary, share your research with the candidate to illustrate that your offer is a proper one, made in good faith.

At some levels, for executives or professionals, the discussions can be far more complicated, going beyond salary to issues such as stock options, a formal employment agreement, and a severance agreement. Sophisticated professionals know that the best time to negotiate a severance agreement is at hiring time. Although that may seem counterintuitive, goodwill is high between parties, everyone is motivated to come to terms, and the astute manager knows that people do get fired for reasons other than cause. Think of the severance agreement as though it were a prenuptial agreement–a good agreement to have in case things do not work out as planned.

Putting the Offer on the Table

You may make a verbal offer of employment, but it is never a done deal until put in writing. You may fax or mail your offer, but do not send it via e-mail. Of course, you may hand the written offer to your candidate at a future meeting.

If the candidate accepts the offer, they should sign the letter to indicate acceptance and to ensure that everyone is clear as to the terms and conditions of employment. Similarly, you should have shared the job description with the employee and adjusted it if necessary based on the negotiations. Make it perfectly clear that the agreement is contingent on a background check and verification of the candidate's stated information, and that any major discrepancies are a firm basis for withdrawing the offer. The agreement should also be contingent on any required drug testing or other screening devices.

The Resources

The Harvard Business Essentials Guide to Negotiations (Harvard Business School Press, 2003) can assist you to improve your general negotiation skills.

Visit your local bookstore or *www.amazon.com*.

17

Drug Testing

Establishing a Drug Free Workplace

The abuse of alcohol and drugs (whether legal or illegal) is a national epidemic. For example, in the United States alone, 73 percent of drug abusers are employed. Related lost productivity and rising health care premiums cost American businesses billions of dollars annually. The chances that your organization employs one or more substance abusers have risen sharply in the past several years. Studies reveal that employees who abuse drugs have a tremendously harmful effect on the workplace: They are more likely to have extended absences from work, show up late, be involved in workplace accidents, and file workers' compensation claims.

In response, employers have established substance abuse programs to respond to the problems created by drugs and alcohol in the workplace. These programs save organizations money, and in some cases they save careers, families and lives. In an effort to raise awareness about the impact of substance abuse in the workplace, the U.S. Department of Labor (DOL) has implemented *Working Partners for an Alcohol- and Drug-Free Workplace.*

The Drug-Free Workplace Act of 1988 was enacted to address the issue of substance abuse in the workplace. This Act requires that contractors and grantees have drug-free workplaces as a precondition to receiving a government contract or grant.

As an employer, you must be concerned about the prevalence of drugs and the abuse of drugs in the workplace. The effect is the same, whether an employee consumes alcohol or drugs on the job, or comes to work under the influence of alcohol or drugs.

The rate of drug abuse is highest among those aged 16 to 25 years of age–the largest age group currently entering the workplace. The Hazelden Foundation has reported that 60 percent of adults personally knew people who have gone to work under the influence of drugs or alcohol.

Pre-Employment Screening

Pre-employment testing has become increasingly popular among employers large and small. There are tests that screen for aptitude, skills, mental health, and drug use. These and other pre-employment screening methods are often used to keep hiring and firing costs to a minimum. As an employer, however, you do not have an automatic right to require testing of prospective employees. You cannot assume the legality of a particular test.

Pre-employment drug screening must be based on sound business principles. Generally, that means that you cannot test simply because you want to; you must have a valid job-related reason for doing so. Such reasons may include the presence of heavy machinery, customer contact, the right of other employees to a drug-free workplace, and lost productivity .

Certain drug testing methods such as urinalysis provide an objective, impartial indication of drug use. Self-reporting, however, in which individuals describe their alcohol or drug-use, is highly subjective and biased. Research has shown that objective drug testing is a more reliable indicator of actual drug use than self-reporting. People are naturally inclined to conceal embarrassing behaviors whenever possible. Objective drug tests reduce the likelihood that recent drug use will go undetected.

Drug tests such as urinalysis detect the presence of most drugs up to 72 hours after the individual has used them. After this window has passed, most drugs become undetectable. Marijuana is an exception to this rule; can be detected in urine for up to 30 days. Most drug tests cannot, however, identify historical use or drug dependence. They can only indicate whether an individual has used a particular drug recently.

Develop a Plan and Communicate Your Policies

Your drug and alcohol use policy should be more than a warning to new employees that you test for drugs and watch for alcohol abuse. You want to advertise in your employee manual that your company is a drug-free environment and that the violation of this policy may be grounds for dismissal.

New employees must be informed that you screen for illegal drugs to the full extent allowed in your state. Furthermore, if your policy includes random drug testing for current employees, make sure your new hires are aware of this policy as well.

Both new hires and current employees should sign a basic form that indicates their consent to drug testing. This ensures that you have not violated their personal or civil rights and that the policy is applied without bias. Indicate that any employment offer, whether verbal or in writing, is conditional upon a clean test. If your company can afford to do so, you should offer assistance to employees who test positive for illegal drugs or excessive alcohol or prescription drug use. Some insurance plans offer at least some remedial help for employees to cope with such dependencies.

Not surprisingly, the federal government is concerned about substance abuse in the workplace and the wider community. The Department of Labor has a partnering program to help businesses take care of these kinds of workplace problems. The Small Business Administration has programs that can assist small business to create drug-free work environments. Financial assistance may be available to small businesses, including free or reduced fees for training sessions; management and supervisor consultations; employee assistance program (EAP) services; and drug testing. Technical assistance may consist of needs assessments; policy and program development; supervisory training on policy enforcement and effective referrals; and consultation on choosing qualified drug testing or EAP service providers.

The Resources

Many of the forms and standard letters needed to manage and enforce a drug testing and drug-free work environment are available at *www.socrates.com* for a fee.

To learn more about the effects of drugs and alcohol on the workplace, visit *www.dol.gov/asp/programs/drugs/workingpartners/stats/wi.asp*. This Website lists extensive statistics on drug and alcohol abuse, some of which are rather shocking. An interactive map at *www.dol.gov/asp/programs/drugs/said/ StateLaws.asp* shows drug-testing regulations by state.

A useful book for employers is *Drug Testing at Work: A Guide for Employers* (Ronin Publishing, 1998), which is available at *www.amazon.com* or other Internet booksellers.

18

Exempt vs. Non-Exempt Employees

Knowing the Difference

You should be clear as to whether a position is classified as exempt or non-exempt before you begin the hiring process. Exempt employees are exempt from Fair Labor Standards Act (FLSA) minimum wage and overtime pay requirements; non-exempt employees are covered under these requirements.

The Department of Labor drafted new regulations on August 23, 2004 regarding the distinctions between the two classifications. The FLSA does not supplant state laws; where states impose additional requirements or restrictions. This means that an exempt position must satisfy the requirements of both federal and state law.

There are three requirements for an exempt position:

1. It must have a minimum salary.
2. It must pay a salaried rather than hourly wage.
3. Its primary duties must be viewed as exempt level duties.

Primary duties are considered an employee's main or most important duties. No absolute percentage of exempt duties is required; however, the lower the percentage, the greater the risk that the position's exempt status will be questioned.

Employee Classifications

There are suggested guidelines for determining whether a job is exempt or non-exempt. The following charts list guidelines for Executive, Administrative, Professional and Sales positions.

Executives

- Primary duty or duties involve management of an enterprise, department or subdivision of an enterprise (50 percent or more of time is a guide).

- Regularly direct two or more full-time employees or equivalent to full-time employees.
- Have hiring and firing authority. To qualify within this guideline, the executive must give recommendations pertaining to employees whom the executive customarily and regularly directs. Occasional suggestions are not enough.
- Use discretionary powers.
- Spend no more than 20 percent of time in non-exempt tasks.

Administration

- Primary duty involves office or non-manual work directly related to management or general business.
- Duties are related to management policies or general business practices.
- Exercise discretion in work and independent judgment on matters of significance.
- May perform special assignments.
- No more than 20 percent of time spent in non-exempt tasks.

Outside Sales

- Primary duty involves making sales or obtaining orders or contracts for services or for the use of facilities for which a consideration will be paid by the client or customer.
- Make sales away from employer's business on a regular and customary basis.
- Spend less than 20 percent of time in non-sales activities.

Professionals (Two types: Learned and Creative)

- Learned
  - Primary duty requires knowledge obtained through prolonged course of study.
  - Work which is intellectual in character.
  - Advanced knowledge must be in a field of science or learning.
  - Use independent judgment.
  - Work must be intellectual and varied, not standard.
- Creative
  - Primary duty requires originality, invention, imagination, or talent in a recognized artistic field.
  - Work can include investigative interviews, writing editorials, opinion columns, or other commentary; analyzing or interpreting public events; and performing on the air in radio, television or other electronic media.

Highly Compensated Employees

The new regulations also define a special exemption for highly compensated employees. This means employees whose salaries are $90,000 or more per calendar or fiscal year. In addition to the salary, these individuals are required to perform at least one of the job duties of an executive, administrative or professional employee.

Non-exempt

Under the new guidelines, most workers quoted a salary less than $23,660 per year or $455 per week, are guaranteed overtime protection and as such are classified as non-exempt employees. All non-exempt positions must be paid overtime for all hours worked in excess of 40 hours in any workweek. Overtime pay is 1.5 times the regular rate of pay.

The FLSA requires that overtime be paid on time worked, not on time compensated. Therefore, no overtime need be paid on sick pay, holiday pay, vacation pay, jury duty pay, or other compensation for days not worked.

Determining a Work Week

A work week is defined as any fixed, recurring period of 168 consecutive hours (24 hours multiplied by 7 days). A work week may begin on any day of the week, but it must be consistent from week to week. A company may have different work weeks for different locations and/or classifications of employees.

Avoiding Problems

To avoid problems and the potential loss of your overtime exemption:

- Update position descriptions.
    - Define the primary duties of the position, not just a series of job tasks.
    - Include supervisory responsibilities.
- Detail the work based upon the exemption status outlined.
    - Know which exemptions you expect and detail the work based upon that type of exemption. For example, an administrative exemption requires the exercise of discretion and independent judgment with respect to matters of significance.
- Keep time sheets for non-exempt personnel.
    - If you do not use a time card system for non-exempt positions, create a time sheet process that your employee signs detailing hours worked for each work week.

- Check to see if flexible schedules meet requirements.
  - Ensure that any flex-time schedules adhere to state and federal laws.
  - Do not trade comp time (time off) for overtime pay.

Employees may ask to take comp time later in the month rather than be paid for overtime. This may seem acceptable, but the law clearly specifies that you must pay overtime for any time worked in excess of 40 hours in one work week.

The Resources

The U.S. Department of Labor provides the *Handy Reference Guide to the Fair Labor Standards Act (FLSA)* at their Website, *www.dol.gov/esa/regs/compliance/whd/hrg.htm.*

The U.S. Office of Personnel Management lists more information about the FLSA in *Making an FLSA Exemption Status Determination—A Work Aid* at *www.opm.gov/flsa/determn.asp.*

19

Non-Compete/ Non-Disclosure Agreements

Protecting Company Information

Non-compete and non-disclosure agreements are written employment contracts frequently used in the course of business. They may be drafted as separate documents or included in a single employment agreement. Not every employee need be expected to sign these types of agreements; they tend to be restricted to upper management, sales people, researchers, and those having access to sensitive and competitive information.

Begin by understanding what these documents are and how they might be used to your company's benefit. A non-compete agreement prevents an employee, after leaving your company, from either starting a competing business or accepting employment with a competitor during a specified period of time. The belief is that if a key employee (for example, a sales manager who has sensitive data about customers) leaves your employ and takes a job with your archrival, he or she has an enormous amount of information about your strategies, finances and other important data. These data in the hands of a competitor could be useful–almost to the point of corporate espionage.

The issue becomes clearer when you examine a list of employees by title who should be asked to sign a non-compete agreement:

- Chief operating officer (other than owner)
- Chief financial manager and senior subordinates
- Sales and marketing managers
- In-house legal counsel
- Researchers, scientists and new product specialists
- Senior designers
- Anyone involved in long-term planning and strategy
- Anyone involved in product improvement, including packaging and contents
- An executive administrator who may have access to important documents and information in the course of his or her duties

It is generally safe to say that janitorial and lower-level clerical employees, customer service representatives, and call-center employees, as well as manufacturing and warehousing employees, are typically not a threat to trade secrets and do not need to sign a non-complete agreement.

When you include this type of document in your hiring process, it is important for your prospective worker to know that he or she is expected to sign such an agreement and the reasons behind it. Further, you do not want to give the impression that signing a non-compete agreement is tantamount to employment for life. You are simply putting reasonable business limits on an employee's actions once leaving your employ.

Limitations on Non-Compete Agreements

While such agreements can give a bit of relief to you as the employer, they are not without problems. Not every state considers such agreements as legal documents. It is important that you do some research or ask your attorney to assist you in the preparation and use of non-compete documents. California, for example, takes a strong position against such agreements, arguing in effect that the law (and non-complete agreements) cannot prevent an individual from making a living in their industry.

Because you have a written agreement with employees, it does not mean that you can arbitrarily restrict future employment. Every state that permits such documents will not enforce them if they are unreasonable. What is considered reasonable and unreasonable, of course, is up for debate. Here are some examples of clauses from unreasonable non-compete agreements:

- Employment restrictions last too long, say 10 years.
- Covers too broad a geographic area, including overseas.
- Too broadly written, meaning not only your current industry but any related industries are restricted.
- Trying to force every employee to sign such an agreement, even though you know that some individuals will never come into important information that could harm your company—back to the janitor again.

In signing such an agreement, employees may ask that you specify a company or two with whom they will not seek employment for a period of time. This approach is a reasonable standard, does not prevent the employee from finding future employment, has a reasonable time limit, and reflects your concerns about your information falling into the hands of your business rivals.

There are many online sources for information and samples of non-complete agreements. There are times when an attorney needs to draft a non-compete agreement for extremely sensitive situations. Keep in mind, you will not be able to enforce your non-complete agreements if you have been inconsistent in enforcing them in the past. If you are going to have this signed document as part of employment or promotion, make sure everyone is treated the same way. Enforce non-compete agreements fairly.

Non-Disclosure Agreements

In general, a non-disclosure agreement follows the general principle that loose lips sink ships. Simply stated, the undisciplined and careless dissemination of important and sensitive company information is not allowed. It is not unreasonable for you as an employer to ask key employees to sign a non-disclosure agreement. It is typically not necessary to have a separate document; this can be part of a general employment agreement or non-compete agreement.

Once again, the reason for using such agreements is based on the assumption that certain employees have access to a sensitive company data. You do not want this information imparted to other companies with whom you are doing business. Imagine negotiating a price increase when your best customer knows your production costs

You as an owner or manager are concerned about reasonable controls on your company's business information. In effect, you are asking employees that during the term of their employment they protect sensitive information in a prudent manner. Some examples of proper due diligence are:

- Taking proper care to file and lock if necessary documents and reports.
- Shred bank statements, internal memoranda and sales reports when no longer needed.
- Sharing information with other employees on a need-to-know basis.
- Not sharing information unnecessarily at events like conferences, industry meetings or even social occasions.
- Not posting or sharing information on the Internet or through e-mails.
- Not leaving printed information where visitors or non-employees can see, read or take them.

The non-disclosure (or confidentiality agreement) is particularly important should an employee leave the company, voluntarily or otherwise. Your agreement should be enforceable after termination in the event that critical information is given out in an inappropriate manner. Your agreement should include specifically the need to return upon leaving the company:

- Disks, files, records, business plans, or other original documents which belong to the company;

- an agreement not to make copies of any documents and then store them at a remote location in any format; and
- the return of all computers and other devices that contain company records, information and telephone numbers.

Some employers are too preoccupied with security, however. There are limits on what can be protected through non-disclosures agreements. For example, an employee cannot be held responsible if certain information is readily available, say to the government or other public bodies. Further, you cannot prevent an employee from providing company information if required in a legal proceeding.

The Resources

An excellent Website with a great deal of information, including sample non-compete agreements, is at *www.toolkit.cch.com/*.

Also, visit *www.socrates.com* for downloadable forms for both non-complete and non-disclosure agreements at moderate prices.

Hiring
Union Employees

Open and Closed Shops

The National Labor Relations Act of 1935 gave most U.S. workers the right to form unions. These organizations give employees the ability to collectively bargain with employers over pay, benefits and working conditions. Unionized and nonunionized companies must abide by the same federal, state and local laws that protect workers' rights. Title VII of the Civil Rights Act of 1964 prohibits employment discrimination based on union membership. Companies must also abide by what is set forth in their collective bargaining agreement with the union(s) representing its workforce.

Open Shops

An open shop does not require union membership as a precondition of employment. Open shops are legally required in right-to-work jurisdictions and by employers such as the federal government. Under U.S. labor law, an open shop may not refuse to hire employees who are members of a union. An open shop may, however, favor nonunion members for employment. The construction industry often enters into prehire agreements, in which the parties agree to draw from a pool of union members, but employers are under no legal obligation to enter into such agreements.

Closed Shops

A closed shop requires union membership as a precondition of employment. The Taft-Hartley Act of 1947 outlawed the closed shop.

Union Shop

A union shop does not require union membership as a precondition of employment. However, union shop employees are required to join the union and pay the equivalent of union dues within an established period of time after hire. Union shops are permitted under the Taft-Hartley Act, except in those states having right-to-work laws. The Act also states that the union cannot force a company to fire an employee for any reason other than failure to pay those dues that are required by all other employees. The Taft-Hartley Act is also known as the Labor-Management Relations Act (LMRA).

Right-to-Work States

A right-to-work law secures the right of employees to decide for themselves whether to join or financially support a union. Employees in the railway or airline industries are not protected by this type of law, and employees of a federal enclave may not be. It is advisable for employers to find out whether their state is a right-to-work state, because that will dictate pertinent union and hiring rights for all parties. Right-to-work laws also differ by state, so it is important to follow the law of your state.

Union Hiring Process

Unionized and nonunionized companies must abide by the same federal, state and local laws that protect workers' rights. The agreed-upon union contract rules and provisions that may affect the hiring process must be taken into account.

An example of how the union contract may affect the hiring process is when company seniority takes precedence for a job that opens in the union shop and is filled by the next senior union member. This may cause the company hiring authority to hire for a lower ranking replacement rather than for the position that was just vacated. Union contracts may also call for the posting of open jobs and job bidding. Posting refers to the practice of notifying existing employees that an opening exists so that interested and qualified employees may apply. Bidding refers to the practice of employees letting management know they are interested in a future opening that does not currently exist. The intention of bidding is to allow management to draw from a pool of candidates who bid for the job. Another union practice that affects hiring is bumping, or giving more senior workers whose jobs have been eliminated the right to transfer into the jobs of less senior workers. Posting, bidding and bumping all affect the hiring process, because the jobs are filled from within the company.

The most important rule of thumb when hiring a union employee is to act in good faith; treat each candidate with honesty and mutual respect. Good practices in the hiring process are relevant in union and nonunion environments. Good hiring practices start with recognizing what knowledge and skills are necessary for a position. Know the laws of your state, do not discriminate against any protected class, and know all the aspects of the collective bargaining agreement that may affect your hiring decision.

The Resources

Visit the Website *www.right-to-work.org* to learn more about detailed information about right-to-work states and laws.

The labor union movement is a particularly colorful part of our business history, often violent and disruptive. If you visit *www.questia.com.library/economics-and-business/business/labor/* you can get all sorts of basic information, including recommended books on the subject as well as additional sites to visits about particular aspects of the labor movement.

21

Determining Wages for New Hires

Always a Difficult Task

Salary administration is always a difficult job. Major corporations and the government have grades or classifications for employees (collective bargaining agreements often include unions in salary administration). The result is that supervisors and managers from large companies have little latitude to determine salary for a new employee. The ranges are set based on work skills, work history and education.

Unfortunately, most owners and managers lack a large enough labor pool or the extensive experience to automatically set salaries. You need to have an attractive compensation plan when hiring employees, good enough to attract quality employees who will stay with the organization. Remember that retention is as important as initial hiring. Turnover is expensive and should be avoided at all costs.

On the other hand, you do not want to pay more than the market rate for employees, especially in basic jobs. Remember that the cost of each employee includes not only gross wages, but also Social Security and Medicare payments, worker's compensation, vacation and sick pay, incentive pay, and benefits such as retirement and healthcare. As a rule, the higher the base salary, the more expensive the benefits and the more costly a potential hiring mistake for the company.

Nothing hurts morale more than when word gets around (and it often does) that a newly hired individual has a higher salary than existing employees doing comparable work. There may be ample reason for the difference, but it is often very hard to justify, especially if the new employee has less experience. And yet, in your mind, this salary is justified because of strong educational background, potential for career growth, or other justifiable business reasons. It can be difficult to balance existing salary schedules and remain competitive in the industry, but even the smallest enterprise can create and manage a rational compensation strategy. It need not be perfect, just reasonable.

Compensation Strategy

In the *plus one* Chapter, *You Need a Body…But Not Just Any Body*, the thrust was to prepare for hiring new and replacement employees by pulling together a comprehensive plan on strategic issues, determining long-term personnel needs for your company, and preparing job descriptions and an employee manual. You can complete this set of documents by spending time with key employees and department heads to get a better understanding of your current payroll/compensation schedule.

Your team has prepared job descriptions for future hires, but you should also have job descriptions for current employees. Ask the employees themselves, with the aid of their manager, to describe their current responsibilities. Each department head should then revise and update these job descriptions to make them as consistent as possible. To make this task easier, create a template which includes the following information:

Company logo
Job Summary/Overview:
Hint:
• insert in bulleted format the most important functions of the job
• use it to sell prospective new employees
Job Functions:
Hint:
• insert in bulleted format the details of the job
• be careful about employment laws, equal employment and protection for the handicapped
Job Requirements:
Hint:
• bulleted list of what is needed, including education, licenses, years experience
• other needs: willingness to travel, reporting relationships, supervisory responsibilities, computer skills, special skills
• work location, work hours
Salary Range:
Hint:
• always give a range
• ensure that these ranges match similar job descriptions
• list benefits, bonuses, vacation and other perks

What Are Your Current Salaries?

To ensure that your compensation strategies for new hires are rational and equitable, it is absolutely necessary that you have a true grasp of what you pay now, to whom and for what type of work. An easy way to do this is to separate exempt from non-exempt employees. Generally speaking, exempt employees are executives, administrators or professionals who supervisor, hire, fire, exercise discretion and/or make significant workplace decisions. All others are non-exempt and must be paid overtime if they work more than 40 hours in a week.

A simple template can simplify the task of tracking compensation. Remember that your total compensation should include wages, bonuses, and any special additions such as parking expenses or company cars for nonbusiness use.

Job Salaries By Exempt And Non-Exempt Employees		
Title	Annualized Salary	Future Hire Salaries
Exempt		
COO/President	$200,000	n.a.
Vice President	$140,000	n.a.
Financial Officer	$120,000	n.a.
Sales Manager		n.a.
Office Manager		
HR Manager		
Operations Manager		
Financial Analyst	$75,000	$75,000 - $80,000
Supervisors/Managers		
IT Manager		
Marketing Manager		
Web Manager		
Warehouse Manager		
Sales		
Other		
Non-exempt		
Executive Assistant	$42,000	$39,000 - $44,000
Receptionist	$26,000	$25,000 - $27,000
Data Entry Clerk	$25,000	$23,000 -$26,000
Department Assistant	$30,000	$29,000 - $32,000
Call Center Level 1		

Call Center Level 2		
Sales Assistant		
Programmer Level 1		
IT Associate		
Warehouse Level 1		
Warehouse Level 2		
Warehouse Level 3		

The primary goal of salary administration is not only to keep tight control on costs, but to ensure that future employees are paid in a similar fashion as current employees. Thus current job descriptions with their embedded salary ranges ensure fairness.

Periodically, as you anticipate hiring additional staff, you will want to know what competitors and companies similar to yours are paying employees. Make every effort to participate in industry or regional salary surveys; often you can get the results of the survey for free or at a greatly reduced price. Find out if your industry association has salary data by job classification. Finally, speak to friends and associates to learn more about their compensation strategies and plans.

The Resources

The rules regarding exempt and non-exempt employment status were changed in 2004, so if you are in doubt, ask for legal help or visit the Department of Labor Website at *www.dol.gov*.

A job description template, which you can customize for your company, is available at *www.encouragementpress.com*. The template for tracking current employee salaries is also found on this Website. You do not need to register, but you are asked to provide an e-mail address on a voluntary basis.

For a more detailed source on job descriptions, visit *www.nolo.com* and consider the book, *Job Description Handbook* (Nolo, 2006). Although useful, it may be more than is needed for small companies and not-for-profit groups.

22

On-Boarding: Integrating New Team Members

Welcoming New Employees

The manner in which newly hired employees are treated when they join an organization often impacts productivity, engagement, retention and motivation. Doing a good job on orienting and socializing new employees will provide benefits to both the organization and the individual.

Benefits to the organization include:

- Reduced turnover
- Clear employee expectations
- Improved job performance
- Enhanced teamwork

Benefits for the individual include:

- Reduced anxiety
- Reduced early employee relations issues
- Increased job satisfaction
- Strengthened cultural alignment

Many organizations do a good job of providing the minimum level of orientation including items such as:

- Work location
- Voicemail and e-mail
- Office supplies
- Facilities

The organizations that do the best job with on-boarding of new employees believe that this process plays a significant role in getting new employees engaged and productive while likely adding significant time to the retention of these employees.

Michael O'Malley, author of the book *Creating Commitment*, says there are two goals for new employee on-boarding: to get people as socially and technically proficient as possible so they can be useful at work and to help them feel like part of the club.

On-boarding differs from what was once known as orientation in two ways. First, on-boarding helps familiarize new employees with their roles, the organization, its policies, and other employees. Second, on-boarding enables socialization to the values, norms and beliefs held by others in the organization.

Here are some ideas for developing your own on-boarding process.

Create a Formal Process that Is also Enjoyable

Outline a program that spans the amount of time required to educate the new hire on important elements of the company: its history, mission, vision, values and senior management. Do not try to do everything in the first few days. Forms are important, but do not overload new employees with forms to complete and manuals to read.

Plan for the new hire and have as much ready as possible on his or her first day. For example, have a working phone, a computer with e-mail, and some initial work available to be completed.

The last thing you want to do is to show long and boring videos or talk about insurance programs when new hires want to engage themselves in their work.

It is impressive to show new hires your on-boarding program outline. Share the steps and the process with them, along with the goals and expectations of each of the steps.

Recognize On-Boarding Programs Take Time

Once the initial up-front stage is completed, it is time to demonstrate how the other stages will be completed and in what time frame. Some companies use a series of cross-functional group assignments to expose the new employee to various facets of the organization while giving them an opportunity to meet and work with different colleagues.

Some organizations create classes of people who are hired within a certain time period and keep them together to have both formal and informal opportunities to engage with each other to build networks that help in the short and long run. This process helps to establish stronger support structures while creating a more fun and relaxing atmosphere for integrating into the organization.

Use Online Tools to Help

Many on-boarding programs today use a blended approach, making information available online so that the new hire and his or her family can learn about the company and the benefits at their convenience. Research has shown that the more engaged the family is to the company, the more difficult the decision to leave. The Internet is a great way to develop a relationship long before the person actually starts in the job. Some companies deliver as much as 40 to 50 percent of their total content via the Internet.

Outline the Manager's Role

Managers are the key to success with any new employee. In fact, it is sometimes said that employees leave managers, not companies. Because the manager has a key role in retaining employees, it is important to clearly understand the role the manager plays in the relationship from the beginning. Be clear about what is expected of employees. Here are some activities that the manager should be responsible for completing with the new hire:

- Greet them on their first day.
- Take them on a tour of the location, department or facility.
- Take them to lunch.
- Introduce the staff.
- Review position description.
- Develop some initial goals and/or work plans.
- Explain policies, agreements and expectations.
- Schedule follow-up discussion dates over 30, 60 and 90 days.

The key to success is to include the manager in both the formal and the informal processes for assimilating new hires into the company.

Create a New Hire Mentor Program

Research conducted on retention indicates that a mentorship relationship outside the direct supervisory role can be beneficial for the employee. A mentor can informally educate the new hire on the company culture. Being a mentor should be considered an important assignment. A mentor should be a good ambassador for the company and an individual that others respect and would like to emulate.

The mentor's role can be both formal and informal. Formal sessions can be outlined with specific objectives to be achieved, while informal aspects could include being available to answer questions or provide advice as requested.

Measure Your Progress

Make sure you constantly measure the progress of your on-boarding program. Be able to determine what aspects of the process are working effectively and what elements could be improved. Everyone seems to have stories about those companies who did a good job of welcoming new hires and those that did not. Learn from your own employees and continue to improve upon your on-boarding process. Do not wait until you start losing your best people to look at the effectiveness of your program.

In summary, the more time and effort spent in helping new employees feel welcome, the more likely they are to identify with the company, its culture, products and people, and thus become more valuable members of the organization. This is reflected later in terms of retention: your employees will find it easy to decline other opportunities because of their commitment to the organization on multiple levels.

The Resources

Visit *www.humancapitalinstitute.org* for a free Webcast series about on-boarding. There are also a number of organizations that offer tools for automating a portion of the on-boarding process; simply search for on-boarding tools on the Internet.

Contract Hiring/
Work-for-Hire

Hire as Needed

The Department of Labor estimates there are eight million contract employees working in the United States today and nearly half of them are not acting in accordance with federal labor guidelines. The IRS requires that workers be correctly classified as employees or independent contractors and imposes significant financial penalties for companies that misclassify workers as independent contractors. Companies may blur the lines when hiring contract employees to meet their specific needs or may simply misinterpret the rules. In either event, companies that are not setting up proper procedures are opening themselves up to future problems. Understanding the IRS's guidelines on what is a contract employee and setting up procedures to ensure you are following the law will encourage successful contract hiring policies.

Do not confuse an employment contract with an independent worker who is under contract to your company. An employment contract is an agreement between the employer and employee that the employment relationship will last for a definitive period of time and can be terminated only for cause or under specified conditions. On the other hand, a bona-fide independent contractor is someone who is running a business, and paid by your company to perform certain work. Such individuals are not employees and they work according to their work contract (work-for-hire agreement). The term of the contract or agreement spells out the exact relationship between the people hired under a contract to perform services.

One of the main reasons for hiring independent contractors is to save money. Many projects are not on-going; you have a specific need or project which cannot justify a full-time employee. As such you contract with an outside individual or company to perform these services. Part of the assumption, even if the project is on-going, is that you save money because you do not have to provide benefits, pay Social Security, purchase equipment and find office space for that person.

The IRS has laid down very specific rules concerning who is an employee and who is an independent contractor. For example:

- Works full time for a company;
- you as the employer determine their work hours;
- if you give specific instructions or training; and
- provide benefits such as health insurance.

The IRS might consider these workers as employees, not independent contractors.

On the other hand, if workers:

- Earn a profit or a loss from their efforts;
- work for many organizations;
- provide their own work place and equipment (computers, supplies);
- do not ask for or seek reimbursement for ordinary expenses;
- determine his own working hours;
- has discretion on how to accomplish the agreed work; and
- is free to hire assistants or other consultants.

Then this is a work-for-hire or contract hiring situation. As an employer, you risk scrutiny from the IRS if you allow contract employees regularly to use your equipment or your facilities for independent work. It then appears as though you are simply trying to avoid FICA and other tax responsibilities.

The Elements of a Contract

A work-for-hire agreement is a document that you and the independent contractor sign that sets the terms of the relationship. It does not have to be a long, complicated document and it can be tailored for any situation. The contract should protect promises made by both parties at the time of signing. The contract describes what the contractor is going to do for you and what you are going to do for the individual. The contract will generally include:

- The nature of the work being offered and accepted.
- The compensation amount to be paid and a schedule of payment.
- The duration of the job (for example: 1 year, 2 years or at-will).
- The specifics of the work/responsibilities.
- When the work is to be completed and how it is to be delivered.
- Whether the work is on-going or for a single project.
- A confidentiality agreement protecting your trade secrets, customer information and client lists.

- Your ownership of the work (for example, if the individual writes books for you or invents products for you, your company owns the copyright or trademark). The employer however, may agree to share with the writer-inventor a percentage of the royalties paid.
- The responsibilities of both parties with regards to the work to be done and the work environment.
- Best-efforts provision states that the contractor promises to work to the best of his or her ability and to be loyal to the employer.
- An exclusivity provision states that the worker promises that as long as he or she works for the company the he will not work for anyone else in the same or similar type of business
- A ground for termination clause states that the employer may terminate the contract for any reason by giving a certain amount of notice, such as 90 days. It may also give the employer the right to just terminate the contract without notice if the contractor violates the contract in any way or becomes permanently disabled due to ill health or physical or mental disability where as he can no longer do the work required.
- An arbitration clause states that both parties agree that if a dispute about any aspect of the work relationship occurs the dispute will be submitted to arbitration rather than seek resolution by a court of law.
- The state from which the dispute will be decided. This part of the contract states that if the parties ever have a dispute that results in a lawsuit, the laws of a particular state, regardless of where the suit is filed or where the company is located, will govern it.
- The agency provision inserted into a contract clearly states that the employer and contractor do not have an employment relationship, no agency relationship meaning the employee has no authority to enter into a contract or otherwise obligate the employer, unless the employer gives express written consent to do so.

The Resources

Visit *http://smallbusiness.findlaw.com* or *www.socrates.com* for more information and sample forms for hiring contract workers. Also, go to the IRS Website for further clarification and information; visit *www.irs.gov*.

Hiring Military

Hiring Veterans Will Serve Your Company

Many job applicants have prior military service or are active in the National Guard or Army Reserve. Long-term service people sometimes have difficulty finding civilian work once they leave the military. The government and veterans' groups work with employers to find and place veterans in suitable employment.

There are a number of benefits to hiring veterans:

- Accelerated learning curve

    Veterans have the proven ability to learn new skills and concepts. In addition, they can enter your workforce with identifiable and transferable skills, proven in real world situations. This background can enhance your organization's productivity.

- Leadership

    The military trains people to lead by example as well as through direction, delegation, motivation and inspiration. Veterans understand the practical ways to manage behaviors for results, even in the most trying circumstances. They also know the dynamics of leadership as part of both hierarchical and peer structures.

- Teamwork

    Veterans understand how genuine teamwork grows out of a responsibility to one's colleagues. Military duties involve a blend of individual and group productivity. They also necessitate a perception of how groups of all sizes relate to each other and an overarching objective.

- Diversity and inclusion in action

    Veterans have learned to work side by side with individuals regardless of race, gender, geographic origin, ethnic background, religion and economic status, as well as mental, physical and attitudinal capabilities. They have the sensitivity to cooperate with many different types of individuals.

- Efficient performance under pressure

Veterans understand the rigors of tight schedules and limited resources. They have developed the capacity to know how to accomplish priorities on time, in spite of tremendous stress. They know the critical importance of staying with a task until it is done right.

- Respect for procedures

Veterans have gained a unique perspective on the value of accountability. They understand their place within an organizational framework, becoming responsible for subordinates' actions to higher supervisory levels. They know how policies and procedures enable an organization to exist.

- Technology and globalization

Veterans are usually aware of international and technical trends pertinent to business and industry. They can bring the kind of global outlook and technological savvy that all enterprises of any size need to succeed.

- Integrity

Veterans know what it means to do an honest day's work. Prospective employers can take advantage of a track record of integrity, often including security clearances. This integrity translates into qualities of sincerity and trustworthiness.

- Conscious of health and safety standards

Thanks to extensive training, veterans are aware of health and safety protocols both for themselves and the welfare of others. Individually, they represent a drug-free workforce that is cognizant of maintaining personal health and fitness. On a company level, their awareness and conscientiousness translate into protection of employees, property and materials.

- Triumph over adversity

In addition to dealing positively with the typical issues of personal maturity, veterans have frequently triumphed over great adversity. They likely have proven their mettle in mission critical situations demanding endurance, stamina and flexibility. They may have overcome personal disabilities through strengths and determination.

Military Leave for Employees

The Uniformed Services Employment and Reemployment Rights Act (USERRA) was created to prevent discrimination specifically against members of the military or the military reserves. This law applies to all private employers no matter how large or small the organization. Most states have similar laws protecting a state militia or its national guard.

The most important issue is that as an employer your actions do not harm an employee because of their active or reservist status in the military. When an individual is called up for active duty and requests a leave for this purpose, it can make staffing difficult, especially if you are a small company. You are not allowed to fire to demote an employee because of military leave, and you must rehire the employee when he or she returns from military service.

The law also states that the individual does not lose seniority while serving in the military. If the employee was entitled to an increase or other benefits, he or she would get these as well. One interesting feature of the law is that you cannot fire a returning employee from military leave without cause for up to 1 year (the exact length depends on years of service as your employee).

USERRA provides protection for disabled veterans by requiring employers to make reasonable efforts to accommodate the disability. Service members convalescing from injuries received during service or training may have up to 2 years from the date of completion of service to return to their jobs or apply for reemployment.

Many employers, recognizing the importance of military service and the hardships such service can create, continue to pay some or all of a person's civilian pay while they are serving the country. The law does not require you to do so, but some partial pay or continuation of some benefits is a gesture of your understanding and respect for your employee.

The Worker also Has Responsibilities

The government recognizes that employees taking military leave, for example, can cause hardship to the employer. In order for workers to receive the protection that USERRA offers, they have responsibilities as well:

- Reasonable notice for military leave must be given to the employer.
- Military leave cannot exceed 5 years.
- The employee must have received an honorable discharge to regain his or her position.

- The employee must report for employment within a reasonable period of time after leaving military service.

The Resources

With nearly 2,000 locations, One-Stop Career Centers help match veterans to your hiring needs. Call 1.877.US2.JOBS or visit *www.servicelocator.org/default.asp* for further information.

For more information about USERRA, visit *www.dol.gov*, then search under veterans. Also visit the Website of Employer Support of the Guard and Reserve at *www.esgr.org*.

25

Reasonable Accommodation Under the Americans with Disabilities Act (ADA)

ADA in the Workplace

In years past, the rights of workers with disabilities were limited, and job opportunities were scarce. It took not only a federal law (the ADA), but also tremendous pressure and a change in public perception and sensitivity, to realize that a worker's physical or mental limitations do not necessarily affect their productivity, creativity and competence.

New technologies have greatly improved opportunities for those with disabilities. The nature of work in all types of industry has changed from physical to intellectual. Physical modifications for automobiles, improved access to public transit systems, and new building standards have improved the ability just to get to work.

Despite the progress that has occurred thus far, some owners and managers remain unable to see the work potential of individuals who have some limitations. While not outwardly violating the law, many skirt the hiring directives concerning employment for the disabled and the related justification to make reasonable accommodations on their behalf. The law was never intended to force employers to hire unqualified workers; in fact, as a rule, all labor laws take a similar slant. If an individual is not qualified for employment, factors protected by law do not come into play.

The ADA went into effect in July 1992 and now applies to employers with 15 or more employees. The law specifically states that it is intended to protect qualified individuals with disabilities from employment discrimination. A qualified individual is one who meets the skill, experience, and educational requirements of a job and who, with or without reasonable accommodations, can perform that job's essential functions.

More than Just Hiring

While your main focus is on hiring and firing, in reality this book and other resources like it cannot isolate these activities from other important personnel matters. In general, the same rules that prevent discrimination for the disabled also prevent discrimination in all areas of employment, including promotion, training, staff development, compensation, reductions in force, freedom from harassment, leaves, fringe benefits and termination.

Companies that have 15 or more employees should establish their personnel policies as part of a planned, written statement, to which all supervisors and employees have access. If this document clearly states that protection under ADA includes more than just hiring and firing, you limit your chances of being sued under the provisions of this law.

Many managers do not know what kinds of disabilities that are covered under this law. The list that follows is merely a guide; it is not intended to be comprehensive nor legally binding.

- cerebral palsy
- muscular dystrophy
- multiple sclerosis
- AIDS
- HIV infection
- emotional illness
- drug (legal) addiction
- alcoholism
- dyslexia

The following are conditions that are not covered under the ADA:

- color of hair or eyes
- pregnancy
- broken bones
- having served a prison sentence
- any temporary impairment

In all cases, when determining if a person has a protected disability, you must make the decision based without regard to mitigating issues such as medication, assisting devices (e.g., cane, crutches) or prosthetic devices (e.g., mechanical arm).

Alcohol and Drugs as Disabilities

At first glance, it may be difficult to understand that both alcohol and drugs could be covered under ADA as legitimate handicaps. Not all employees who use drugs or alcohol are automatically disabled under the law. For example, an individual currently using illegal drugs is not considered disabled under the law and is not covered by it. However, workers who are currently in a drug rehabilitation program, or who have completed such a program, are covered, provided that they abstain from future illegal drug use.

You may need to accommodate employees who are disabled by side effects of legal drugs. You need not have different or special standards for these employees; they can follow the same standards applied to all other employees, such as not using drugs or alcohol on the job, being on time, meeting reasonable productivity standards, and so forth.

Making Reasonable Accommodation

Making reasonable accommodation for prospective handicapped employees is common sense. What you as an employer or supervisor think is reasonable may be very different from what applicants and the Department of Labor consider reasonable. The norm for accommodation is as follows: modification or an adjustment to a job or the work environment that will enable a qualified applicant or employee with a disability to perform the essential job functions.

The term essential job function refers to a primary job duty that a qualified individual must be able to perform. It may be considered essential because it is a key job requirement or because it is highly specialized. Some examples of reasonable accommodation are:

- adjusting the height of a desk or work surface to accommodate a wheelchair
- telephone equipment that assists a hearing-impaired worker
- a quiet work environment for individuals with attention deficit disorders
- a large-screen monitor for individuals with poor vision
- making your offices or plant accessible to the handicapped (assuming you own the property)
- job restructuring
- magnifying glass
- headset instead of a traditional telephone receiver
- modifying work schedules
- modifying training materials to assist the handicapped (large print)
- changing work schedules to part-time from full-time

It is the employee's responsibility to tell you that he or she needs an accommodation. The law does not require you as an employer to realize that there is a need. But once you are informed of a problem, you cannot pretend that you did not know about it because you are unwilling to be flexible or make changes. It is your responsibility to engage employees in discussions about how they may be reasonably accommodated on the job.

Undue Hardship to an Employer

The spirit and practice of the ADA is to make employment available to individuals with disabilities. It is not intended to be punitive or put undue demands on employers who cannot reasonably manage the challenges of accommodating such individuals. Here are examples of undue hardship that the government would consider reasonable:

- accommodation would be excessively expensive
- the size and financial resources of your organization
- if the changes would be excessively disruptive
- how your business is structured

If you are unable to accommodate a disabled individual in a reasonable manner, and if the employee offers to pay for the cost of accommodation, you cannot legally turn down the offer.

Three tax incentives are available to help businesses offset the costs of accommodations and improve employment opportunities for employees with disabilities.

- The Small Business Tax Credit (IRS Code Section 44, Disabled Access Credit) can be used by certain small businesses for architectural changes, equipment or services such as sign language interpreters.
- The Architectural/Transportation Tax Deduction (IRS Code Section 190, Barrier Removal) can be used by businesses of any size to make architectural and transportation modifications.
- The Work Opportunity Tax Credit (WOTC) benefits certain employers who hire certain targeted low-income groups, including Social Security Insurance recipients or certified vocational rehabilitation referrals.

The Resources

A useful resource is the *Federal Employment Laws: A Desk Reference* (Nolo, 2002). You can purchase both print and electronic versions at *www.nolo.com*.

For more information about compliance with ADA and the tax incentives available to businesses, visit the U.S. Department of Labor Office of Disability Employment Policy's publication page at *www.dol.gov*.

26

Affirmative Action–
Who Needs It &
Where Is It Now?

Laws Protecting Workers from Discrimination

In 1965 President John F. Kennedy signed Executive Order 10925 establishing the President's Committee on Equal Employment Opportunity (EEOC). This committee was directed to study employment practices of the U.S. government and to consider and recommend steps to correct past discrimination hiring practices and to prevent such discriminations in the future.

The phrase affirmative action was first used in President Lyndon Johnson's Executive Order 11246 of 1965. This required federal contractors to take affirmative action to ensure that applicants are employed, and that employees are treated during employment, without regard to their race, creed, color or national origin. The practice of affirmative action is no longer limited to federal contractors; most states and companies have some form of affirmative action in force. Institutions with affirmative action policies generally set goals and timetables for increased diversity and use recruitment, set-asides and preferences as ways of achieving those goals.

Affirmative action policies focus particularly on the areas of education, employment, government contracts, health care and social welfare. These policies require that active measures be taken to ensure that African Americans, Hispanics, Latinos, Native Americans, Asian-Americans, and other minorities enjoy the same opportunities for promotions, salary increases, career advancement, school admissions, scholarships, and financial aid. The purpose of the Act is to increase the representation and opportunities for those groups that have traditionally experienced discrimination. From the outset, affirmative action was developed as a temporary remedy expected to be no longer needed once there was a level playing field for all Americans. In 1967 Johnson expanded the executive order to include affirmative action requirements to benefit women.

According to the Department of Labor, companies have significantly changed the corporate climate as a direct result of the requirements of affirmative action and other laws. For example, corporations now post job announcements and do not rely solely on word of mouth recruitment. Corporate sensitivity to issues like sex and race harassment and wage discrimination has increased, as has the awareness of the benefits of a family-friendly environment. Employers now view ability, not disability.

Laws that have been adopted as a result of affirmative action include:

- Reverse Discrimination
- Title VII of the Civil Rights Act of 1964
- Equal Pay Act of 1963
- Age Discrimination in Employment Act of 1967 (ADEA)
- Rehabilitation Act of 1973, Sections 501 and 505
- Titles I and V of the Americans with Disabilities Act of 1990 (ADA)
- Civil Rights Act of 1991

Reverse Discrimination in the Workplace

In its modern form, affirmative action may produce reverse discrimination. This is a term that describes policies or habits of social discrimination against members of a historically dominant group with an implication of unfairness. Reverse discrimination, whether intentional or unintentional, causes the dominant group to become the disadvantaged minority. It happens, for example, when an admissions officer or hiring manager is faced with two similarly qualified applicants of different groups. The hiring manager may choose the minority over the non-minority, or recruit and hire a qualified woman instead of a man.

Affirmative action decisions are generally not supposed to be based on quotas, nor are they supposed to give any preference to unqualified candidates. They are also not supposed to harm anyone through reverse discrimination. The Civil Rights Act of 1965 says that all people are protected from all forms of employment discrimination based on sex, race, national origin and the like. There have been numerous reverse discrimination court cases over the years. Courts now recognize that all individuals are protected by the statute, even white males. The law, as interpreted by courts, is that any person who benefits from affirmative action in the workplace must have relevant job and educational qualifications.

Sexual Orientation Discrimination

Sexual orientation discrimination is a bias against individuals, couples or groups based on sexual orientation, whether real or perceived. Usually, this involves those who have a same-sex sexual orientation, whether gay, lesbian or bisexual.

Sexual minorities are often seen as undesirable or immoral by one or more social groups; as a result, discrimination against them is frequently codified in state statutes. As acceptability of sexual orientation varies greatly from society to society, the degree to which discrimination is sanctioned by society also varies greatly. Discrimination based on sexual orientation is often exacerbated by frustration or anger brought about societal changes that seem threatening to some members of society. In the United States, 17 states have banned discrimination based on sexual orientation, with most laws focusing on freedom from discrimination in housing, public accommodations and the workplace. Most of these states exempt religious institutions from these anti-discrimination clauses, and several exempt small businesses.

Religious Discrimination

Religious discrimination is a bias for or against a particular faith group. Religious students may be said to be discriminated against in some western state schools. Names of clubs have been changed due to claims by administrative staff that some part of the name or the symbolism it represents may offend some students, parents or teachers.

Gender Discrimination

Gender discrimination is any action that grants or denies opportunities, privileges or rewards to a person on the basis of their sex. The United Nations has stated that women often experience a glass ceiling and that there are no societies in which women enjoy the same opportunities as men. The term glass ceiling is the invisible barrier that effectively bars women from promotion in certain companies. In the United States, the Glass Ceiling Commission notes that between 95 and 97 percent of senior managers in the country's largest corporations are men. Transgendered individuals often experience gender discrimination because of their identity.

Sexual differences have been used to justify societies in which one sex has been restricted to significantly inferior and secondary roles. While there are nonphysical differences between men and women, there is little agreement as to what those differences are. Legislation to promote gender equality is generally complex and varied, with a wide divergence among different countries.

Age Discrimination

Age discrimination is a bias against a person or group on the basis of age, but typically affects youth and the elderly. In many countries, companies openly refuse to hire people above a certain age, despite the ever-increasing life expectancy and average age of the population. Reasons range from vague feelings that younger people are more dynamic and create a positive image for the company, to more concrete concerns about regulations granting older employees higher salaries or other benefits without these expenses being fully justified by an older employees' greater experience.

Sexual Discrimination

Title VII of the Civil Rights Act of 1964 protects individuals against employment discrimination on the basis of sex as well as race, color, national origin and religion. Title VII applies to employers with 15 or more employees and includes state and local governments. It also applies to employment agencies, labor organizations and the federal government. It is unlawful to discriminate against any employee or applicant for employment because of his or her sex in regard to hiring, termination, promotion, compensation, job training, or any other term, condition, or privilege of employment. Title VII also prohibits employment decisions based on stereotypes and assumptions about abilities, traits, or the performance of individuals on the basis of sex. Title VII prohibits both intentional discrimination and neutral job policies that disproportionately exclude individuals on the basis of sex and that are not job related.

Title VII's prohibitions against sex-based discrimination also cover:

- Sexual harassment. This includes practices ranging from direct requests for sexual favors to workplace conditions that create a hostile environment for persons of either gender, including same sex harassment.
- Pregnancy-based discrimination. Title VII was amended by the Pregnancy Discrimination Act, which prohibits discrimination on the basis of pregnancy, childbirth and related medical conditions.

The Resources

The Department of Labor provides an overview of affirmative action at *www.dol.gov/esa/regs/compliance/ofccp/aa.htm*.

The American Association for Affirmative Action at *www.affirmativeaction.org* is a non-profit organization dedicated to advocating affirmative action enhancements in the workplace. The Website *www.inmotionmagazine.com/aahist.html* displays a timeline of the evolution of affirmative action policies in the United States.

27

Bona Fide Occupational Qualifications

Understanding the Basics

A bona fide occupational qualification (BFOQ) is a defense to acknowledged discrimination, usually based on the existence of a facially discriminatory policy (e.g., individuals over the age of 50 shall not be hired as police officers). Title VII permits you to discriminate on the basis of religion, sex, or national origin only in those instances where religion, sex, or national origin is a bona fide occupational qualification that is reasonably necessary to the normal operation of the particular business or enterprise. This narrow exception has also been extended to discrimination based on age through the Age Discrimination in Employment Act (ADEA). This exception does not apply to discrimination based on race.

Whether a particular policy amounts to a BFOQ requires an analysis of the facts of each particular case. The Equal Employment Opportunity Commission (EEOC) maintains a list of approved BFOQs, but this list is only a guideline. The question of whether a policy is a BFOQ is a factual determination for the court.

In determining whether a discriminatory policy constitutes a BFOQ, you must first look at the particular job and what it requires. Then examine the discriminatory policy and determine if it is necessary to performing the job. For example, the Federal Aviation Administration (FAA) has a rule that prohibits an airline pilot from serving as a captain after reaching the age of 60. This rule is based on the probability that a pilot's skills deteriorate with age and that the safety of the crew and passengers depends most heavily on the captain. This rule only pertains to the position of captain; pilots 60 years of age or older are not precluded from serving as flight engineers because age is not a BFOQ for the position of flight engineer.

In claiming the defense of BFOQ, the employer has the burden of proving that the discriminatory policy is a valid BFOQ. The employer must demonstrate plainly and unmistakably that its discriminatory employment practice meets the terms and spirit of the Title VII exception. In other words, the employer must demonstrate that a discriminatory practice is reasonably related to an essential operation of the business. There is no requirement that formal studies be conducted to ascertain the need for a BFOQ. A BFOQ can be demonstrated through the use of expert witnesses, empirical data or simple common sense.

BFOQ and Age Discrimination

The courts have developed a two-step test for analyzing BFOQ defenses in dealing with policies that preclude a certain age group from a job. An employer must show either (1) that there is a substantial basis for believing that all or nearly all employees above a certain age lack the qualifications for the position in question; or (2) that reliance on an age classification is necessary because it is highly impractical for the employer to insure by individual testing that its employees will have the necessary qualifications for the job. These BFOQs usually apply to jobs involving driving, flying or physically demanding jobs.

BFOQ and Gender Discrimination

While BFOQs related to gender discrimination do not have a specific two-step test, the analysis does require that the discriminatory practice is reasonably necessary to the normal operation of a particular business or enterprise. In other words, gender discrimination is valid only when the essence of the business operation would be undermined if the business eliminated its discriminatory policy.

For example, corrections facilities and mental institutions which maintain gender specific wards usually have rules requiring at least one staff member of the same gender as the patients to always be on duty. This policy was found to be a valid BFOQ because the privacy rights of the individual patients necessitated that a staff member of the same sex be available to assist patients in toileting, showering and disrobing. Another example would be the argument that the essence or identity of a restaurant is based on its exclusive employment of female waitresses and bartenders, and the business would be undermined if it were forced to hire male waiters and bartenders.

Surprisingly, concern for the safety of its female employees is not a recognized BFOQ. For example, a battery manufacturer enacted a policy prohibiting women who were pregnant or of child-bearing age from working in jobs that involved exposure to lead. The purpose of this rule was to protect against any risk of harm to potential children of female employees. While this policy was well intended, it was found to be illegal because the policy was not reasonably necessary to the normal production of batteries. To put it another way, fertile women were as efficient in the manufacturing of batteries as anyone else.

The Resources

Two very helpful documents from the Federal government include *Employer EEO Responsibilities: Preventing Discrimination in the Workplace, Revised Edition* (written by the EEOC Technical Assistance Program) and *Age Discrimination: Employment Discrimination Prohibited by the Age Discrimination in Employment Act of 1967* (Also written and amended by the EEOC) can be found at *www.dol.gov*.

28

Knowing the Law When Firing Employees

Knowing the Facts

This chapter uses the word firing to mean the involuntary termination of an employee. Poor job performance, cause and layoffs are valid reasons for firing an employee. Poor job performance is grounds for firing when an employee fails to meet the performance standards set by the company. Violation of company policy such as theft, fighting, or falsification of credentials is grounds for firing for cause. Layoffs as a result of budget cuts, economic slowdowns, or poor financial conditions are also valid reasons for firing.

There are a number of state and federal laws and doctrines that have been passed to protect the rights of employees and employers with respect to firing. Title VII of the Civil Rights Act of 1964 prohibits discrimination in hiring, transfers, promotions, compensation, access to training, and other employment related decisions. Title VII rights afforded an employee in the hiring process cannot be legally violated and must be adhered to in the firing process. The violation of Title VII rights during a firing is unlawful, results in wrongful discharge, and invites litigation.

Other key laws to be addressed and followed when firing an employee are:

- The Civil Rights Act of 1991, which provides damage awards to individuals who have been intentionally discriminated against in violation of Title VII, the Americans with Disabilities Act, and the Rehabilitation Act.
- The Age Discrimination in Employment Act of 1967, which prohibits discrimination in hiring and firing against persons over 40 years of age. The act prohibits treatment of employees because of their age in any way that adversely affects their employment status. The act covers all private and public employers with 20 or more employees, all unions with 25 or more employees, and all employment agencies, apprenticeships and training programs.

- The Rehabilitation Act of 1973, which prohibits discrimination based on physical or mental disabilities. Employers are not required to employ unqualified people.
- The Americans with Disabilities Act of 1990, which applies to companies with 15 or more employees. The act protects qualified individuals with disabilities from discrimination in the workplace inclusive of training and career development.
- The Pregnancy Discrimination Act of 1978, which makes it illegal to refuse to hire a woman because she is pregnant or to fire a woman because she is pregnant.
- The Family Medical Leave Act of 1993, which prohibits companies from firing employees who exercise their right to take up to 12 weeks unpaid time off in a 12-month period. Employees are eligible for family leave due to the birth of a child; the adoption of a child or foster care placement; a serious health condition that makes an employee unable to perform their job; or a serious health condition affecting a spouse, child or parent for whom the employee must provide care. The act applies to companies employing 50 or more employees within a 75-mile radius.

It is imperative that companies give careful consideration to the above laws so that they do not violate the rights of any individual or protected class in their decision to fire an employee.

A number of states follow the employment-at-will doctrine, which means that an employee hired for an indefinite period of time may be terminated for any or no reason, cause or no cause. However, an employer may not terminate an individual in violation of state or federal law.

It is always best to follow a well-documented progressive disciplinary process when dealing with employee performance, incidents or behavior that may lead to firing. When the decision is made to fire an employee, he or she is entitled to all accrued vacation pay as well as COBRA, unless the firing results from gross misconduct.

COBRA

The Consolidated Omnibus Budget Reconciliation Act of 1985 (COBRA) requires employers who provide health care coverage and who employ more than 20 people to allow for the continuation of health care coverage to employees, their spouses, their former spouses, and their dependent children in the event that such coverage would end due to certain qualifying events. Qualifying events include:

- Death of a covered employee;
- termination or reduction in hours of a covered employee for any reason other than gross misconduct;
- divorce or legal separation from a covered employee;
- a covered employee becoming entitled to Medicare; and
- a child's loss of dependent status (and there for coverage) under the plan.

COBRA allows individuals who would otherwise lose their health care coverage due to a COBRA qualifying event to continue their coverage for 18 to 36 months, and sometimes longer. The premiums for the continued health care are the responsibility of the individual. Employers may require those who elect continuation to pay the full cost of coverage, plus a 2 percent administrative charge. The length of time coverage continues is determined by the type of qualifying event as listed below:

Event	Months of continued coverage
Termination of employment for any reason other than gross misconduct	18
Reduction in hours	18
Employee is disabled at the time of reduction in hours or termination	29
Divorce or death of employed spouse	36
Loss of eligibility by dependent child	36

COBRA coverage usually stops when the individual stops paying premiums, finds another job with benefits, or gains Medicare coverage, or if the company goes out of business.

Sexual Harassment

Title VII of the Civil Rights Act of 1964 prohibits discrimination on the basis of gender. Federal courts have ruled that sexual harassment is a form of gender discrimination. The Equal Employment Opportunity Commission (EEOC) guidelines issued initially in 1978 hold the employer responsible for the actions of its employees. The EEOC guidelines define sexual harassment as unwelcome sexual advances, requests for sexual favors, and other verbal or physical conduct of a sexual nature. Conduct constitutes sexual harassment when submission to such conduct is made a condition of employment, is used as the basis for employment decisions, and has the purpose of interfering with work performance or creating an intimidating, hostile, or offensive work environment.

Sexual harassment claims fall in two categories:

- Quid pro quo (or this for that) harassment occurs when an employee is forced to choose between submission to the sexual demands of a superior and giving up an economic benefit like a pay increase, a promotion, or continuation of employment.
- Hostile environment harassment takes place when sexual or other discriminatory behavior interferes with an employee's ability to perform his or her job. A hostile environment is one in which the work environment is threatening, intimidating or humiliating or adversely affects the employee's psychological well being. Hostile environment sexual harassment can be created by supervisors, coworkers or by non-employees such as customers.

Firing an Employee for Sexual Harassment

It is the employer's responsibility to protect its employees against all forms of sexual harassment through appropriate intervention, including progressive discipline inclusive of involuntary termination. It is recommended that companies have a sexual harassment policy in place and clearly state that violators are subject to being fired.

How to Avoid Litigation from Sexual Harassment

Employers are vicariously liable for the wrongful actions of their employees, so it is essential that employers take appropriate action to insure that all forms of sexual harassment are not tolerated in the workplace. Employers can reduce their liability and avoid litigation by taking the following positive actions:

- Publish a written anti-harassment policy.
- Publish a written harassment prevention program.
- Communicate the anti-harassment policy and prevention program to all employees.
- Define what constitutes sexual harassment and state that it will not be tolerated.
- Establish a complaint procedure.
- Encourage employees who are victims or witnesses to come forward.
- Thoroughly investigate every complaint (prevents litigation from either party).
- If the investigation shows that sexual harassment occurred, take progressive disciplinary action including firing.
- Put in place preventive mandatory measures such as training and education programs for all employee levels.
- Communicate the policy through the handbook, postings and oral communication.

- Keep records on who was trained and cover every employee, especially new ones.

Numerous states require supervisory training on sexual harassment by statute or by case law, and all states will eventually mandate such training. The employer who voluntarily protects the rights of its employees to work in an environment free from sexual harassment also protects itself from litigation.

The Resources

Visit the Society for Human Resource Management (SHRM) Website at *www.shrm.org*.

State specific employment at-will information is available at the U.S. Department of Labor Website at *www.bls.gov/opub/mlr/2001/01/art1full.pdf*.

Other useful Websites in this subject area are the U.S. Department of Labor at *www.dol.gov/dol/topic/health-plans/cobra.htm* and the U.S. Equal Employment Opportunity Commission at *www.eeoc.gov*.

Wrongful Termination

Avoiding Wrongful Termination and Its Consequences

Deciding to terminate an employee is never easy. Before you make that final decision, you and your human resources department need to review objectively all the facts and discuss the situation with your employment attorney. There are circumstances under which you absolutely cannot terminate an employee, no matter how badly you would like to, because doing so would be a violation of the law. There are other situations where firing the employee would not necessarily be against the law, but would most likely provoke legal action against you. Both these types of situations are considered wrongful termination and should be avoided. The term describes situations where an employee has been fired, believes the decision to be unjust, and then sues the employer. In many of these cases, the action to fire clearly violates the law.

All states are covered by federal legislation, which includes illegal discrimination and other employment laws. Most states are also covered by state and local legislation, which typically expands the scope and range of the federal laws. By their very nature, laws that prevent discrimination inherently and explicitly prevent wrongful termination. These laws have their origins in the following federal acts:

- Title VII of the Civil Rights Act of 1964 (Title VII), which prohibits employment discrimination based on race, color, religion, sex, or national origin.
- The Age Discrimination in Employment Act of 1967 (ADEA), which protects individuals who are 40 years of age or older.
- Titles I and V of the Americans with Disabilities Act of 1990 (ADA), which prohibit employment discrimination against qualified individuals with disabilities in the private sector and in state and local governments.
- Sections 501 and 505 of the Rehabilitation Act of 1973, which prohibit discrimination against qualified individuals with disabilities who work in the federal government.

- Civil Rights Act of 1991, which, among other things, provides monetary damages in cases of intentional employment discrimination.

The Equal Employment Opportunity Commission (EEOC) is responsible for enforcing these laws. An employee who believes he or she was wrongfully terminated will usually first seek assistance from the EEOC. There are other laws which prohibit reprisal and discrimination which are not in the domain of the EEOC. These include:

- Federal Bankruptcy Act, which protects employees from discrimination at the workplace if they have sought protection under the bankruptcy code.
- The Civil Service Reform Act, which protects federal employees from discrimination based upon race, color, national origin, religion, sex, age, disability, marital status, political affiliation, or sexual orientation. It also contains a retaliation provision that protects employees if they chose to exercise their appeal, complaint or grievance rights.
- The Whistleblower Protection Act, an amendment to the Civil Service Reform Act. This act specifically protects all employees from retaliation if they report an employer's illegal behavior to authorities. The seven major environmental laws (Atomic Energy, Clean Air, Clean Water, Safe Drinking Water, Solid Waste, Superfund, and Toxic Substances) specifically mention whistleblowing and contain specific language to protect employees who report illegal actions.

These laws cover a multitude of situations and are designed to protect the employee from discriminatory and retaliatory action taken by an employer. It is illegal to fire any employee if he or she is covered by any of the laws listed above. These laws were put in place gradually over the past 50 years to help employers remain honest and treat their employees fairly. If you choose to fire someone that falls into one of the categories above, you run a huge risk of being hit with a lawsuit and in all probability losing the case. The consequences are likely to be more than just losing the lawsuit and paying large sums of money both to the plaintiff and to the attorney who is defending you. You also run the risk of incurring a large fine and damaging your reputation inside and outside the company. Defending these types of lawsuits takes incredible amounts of time and money, and are usually a lose-lose situation for any business. No matter how much you want to get rid of an employee, you cannot risk a wrongful termination suit–especially one you are almost certain to lose.

Potential wrongful termination cases include situations in which:

- The employee is pregnant;
- you would like to replace an older worker with a younger one;
- the employee reported illegal or immoral activity on your premises;

- the employee is bankrupt;
- the employee is recovering from a life-threatening illness;
- the employee took off time to vote;
- the employee lied when asked about union activity (you are not entitled to ask about union activity); and
- you object to an employee's support of a particular political party.

Laws have becoming increasingly more aggressive in protecting employee's rights. Some wrongful termination scenarios do not violate any state or federal laws, but they are few. These are situations that are not necessarily covered under federal, state or local law, but can still provoke legal action.

Examples of common employer mistakes:

- Breaking a stated or understood promise.
- If the employee received a favorable review within the last 3 to 6 months, it is likely that the employee will feel very betrayed if terminated suddenly.
- Firing an employee because you do not like the employee's attire and you never communicated that to him or her.
- Leading an employee to believe that you can only fire him or her for cause or flagrant offenses.
- Firing impulsively, without careful research and investigation.
- Discussing the termination with other employees.
- Firing a long-term employee without sufficient opportunities for improvement or coaching.
- Walking the employee out dramatically and/or not letting the employee pack his or her belongings.
- Giving a negative reference to future employers.

Preventing Problems

These mistakes can be avoided by planning and by applying good business sense to employer-employee relations. A terminated employee who believes that he or she was treated fairly is much less likely to seek legal redress. The employee will also be disinclined to sue if he or she does not think the case is winnable.

Some common-sense considerations will go a long way in helping you avoid litigation:

- Documentation
  - This cannot be emphasized enough. If you have documented the employee's misconduct or poor performance, the employee will be less likely to sue because he or she will know that they are unlikely to prevail in court.
  - Of course, another obvious advantage to documentation is that this is critical to helping you win in court if the employee does sue.

- Communication
  - Make sure your policies are spelled out in your employee manual and that your employee has signed off on them. This way, your employee cannot plead ignorance when a particular performance issue comes up.
  - No one likes surprises. If you are unhappy with your employee's performance for any reason, say so. Tell the employee orally or in writing or both, but be clear that there are problems as soon as the problems arise, so the employee is not blindsided.
- Fairness
  - Does the punishment fit the crime? Have the offenses been so egregious as to truly warrant termination of the relationship? Remember, you have invested a great deal of time and money in training this employee. Do not forget to consider the possibility that perhaps the relationship can be saved.
  - Have you treated all employees equally? Have all employees in the same position or same level been treated the same? Were they each allowed the same amount of personal calls, flexibility in hours, allowances for miscues or mistakes?
  - Have you considered whether there are any outside extenuating circumstances that could explain the employee's poor performance? Perhaps the employee's mother or father is facing a life-threatening illness or the employee is undergoing a lifestyle change.

Most employees take a job intending to do their best. They typically expect to do the work and be rewarded fairly. In a similar vein, employers hire staff with the highest expectations and the understanding that this will be a win-win scenario for both the new employee and the company. Unfortunately, things do not always work out this way. Your job as the employer is to make certain that when an employee must be terminated, the situation is handled with dignity both for the employee's sake and for your own.

The Resources

The EEOC's Website (*www.eeoc.gov*) contains the entire text of the acts discussed in this chapter.

The best way to avoid lawsuits is to make sure you have a competent human resources staff, as well as an attorney knowledgeable in employment law. Ask your business associates and fellow business owners for attorney referrals.

Another option is to check any of the following Websites: *www.martindale.com*, *www.findlaw.com* and *www.lawyers.com*.

Employment At-Will

Understand the Meaning of At-Will Employment

How do you protect yourself and your company from being sued by a terminated employee? In most states, companies are protected under the employment at-will doctrine, which states that: An employee not under contract is considered an at-will employee, and employment is presumed to be voluntary and indefinite. To date 38 states have adopted the employment at-will doctrine.

An employer can dismiss an employee hired for an indefinite term at any time for any nondiscriminatory reason and without consequence. Employees may be fired for any number of job-related or non job-related reasons such as behaving inappropriately at the company dinner, irritating the employer or simply answering the phone the wrong way one day. Conversely, an at-will employee is free to terminate his or her employment at any time for any reason and without consequence.

While it may seem one-sided that an employer may willy-nilly fire employees for real or imagined reasons, the doctrine lists three exceptions for employer and employee to follow:

1. Employers cannot violate state or federal laws, and generally cannot rightfully terminate employees who refuse to do something that is contrary to public policy and sound morality, such as breaking the law. Forty-three U.S. states recognize public policy as an exception to the at-will rule. Under the public policy exception, an employer may not fire an employee if it would violate the state's public policy or any state or federal statute. Most at-will states look to public policy to be within the spirit of the state constitution, statute or administrative rule. In other words, each state interprets public policy differently.

2. Termination is prohibited after an implied contract for employment has been established, either in the form of oral assurances or expectations created by employer handbooks, policies or other written assurances.

3. Termination in bad faith or with intentional malice is prohibited. A small number of states include an implied covenant of good faith and fair dealing in the employment relationship in order to prevent malicious firings.

Although some employers interpret it as such, employment at-will does not allow employers to terminate employment on a whim. According the Uniform Law Commissioners, an avalanche of lawsuits in the 1980s significantly weakened the employment at-will doctrine, thereby forcing the creation of the Model Employment Termination Act (META). While employment is still at-will for employers and employees, states that have adopted META now require employers, at a minimum, to at least show good cause for terminating an employee. Good cause is any legally justifiable or legitimate business reason, such as layoff or misconduct.

A state that has not adopted META may already have a related law on the books. An employment at-will agreement or employee policy manual might define good cause for termination, but good cause is often a matter of interpretation by the court or an arbitrator. For example, if you fire an employee for allegedly violating a company policy, and the employee contests the termination, a court might consider one or more of the following to determine whether you had good cause to terminate the employment:

- You made the employee aware of the policy infraction and warned him or her about the consequences of violating it again.
- You gave the employee a chance to explain his or her side of the story.
- You can successful argue that the policy is not frivolous and that ignoring the policy may hurt the company or other employees.
- The employee has a poor attendance or review record with the company.
- The employee and other employees have been disciplined for similar violations.
- The policy was in place before an employee violated it.
- Termination for good cause is listed in the employee handbook or similar document.

The employment at-will doctrine is so vigorously protected that courts have upheld it on occasion despite the fact that employers have proved only weak cause for termination. As long as an employer does not violate other laws, the courts tend to uphold the at-will doctrine.

Not all employees are protected by the at-will doctrine:

- Most state and federal government employees are not defined as at-will employees, and can be demoted or fired only for such cause as will promote the efficiency of the service. All federal employees are protected from any termination that violates the U.S. Constitution or the constitution of the state in which they work. For example, an employee's rights to freedom of speech, association, religion, or freedom from unlawful search and seizure may be at issue when an employee is terminated.

- Members of most labor unions are covered by a written contract or collective bargaining agreement with a clause specifying that employment can be terminated only for just cause. Employees covered under an employment contract can only be terminated as the contract permits. If an employer fails to follow the contract regarding terminating or disciplinary action, an employee may have a breach of contract claim.

A number of federal laws have been passed in an effort to reduce abuse from the employment at-will doctrine and to help enforce good cause terminations. Your state might have laws that supplement or modify the following federal laws below. Federal laws typically mandate only the minimum compliance for employers in all states, allowing individual states to enact their own labor laws. Contact your state's EEOC employment office for additional information.

- Fair Labor Standards Act (FLSA)
- Age Discrimination In Employment Act of 1967 (ADEA)
- Americans with Disabilities Act of 1990 (ADA), Titles I and V
- Bankruptcy Act of 1978, Section 525(b)
- Civil Rights Act of 1964, Title VII
- Civil Service Reform Act of 1978
- Consumer Credit Protection Act of 1968
- Employee Polygraph Protection Act of 1988
- Employee Retirement Income Security Act of 1974 (ERISA)
- Fair Credit Reporting Act of 1999 (FCRA)
- Family & Medical Leave Act of 1993 (FMLA)
- Immigration Reform & Control Act of 1986, Title 8
- Judiciary and Judicial Procedure Act of 1948
- Mine Safety and Health Act of 1977, Section 815(c)
- Railroad Safety Act of 1970, Section 20109
- Rehabilitation Act of 1973, Sections 501 and 505
- Uniformed Services Employment and Reemployment Rights Act of 1994 (USERRA)
- Vietnam Era Veterans' Readjustment Assistance Act of 1974
- Whistleblower Protection Act

Protect yourself and your company. The best way to preserve your at-will employment relationship with employees is to be clear about the relationship in your offer letter. Spell out the major terms and conditions of employment, such as reporting relationships, scope of duties, compensation, benefits, confidentiality and protection of trade secrets.

A good, clear offer letter may read like:

> Dear Jerry:
>
> Welcome aboard! We look forward to developing our relationship with you and hope you view this opportunity as a chance to have a long-term positive impact on our business. Nonetheless, please understand that XYZ Company is an at-will employer, meaning that either the company or the employee is free to end the employment relationship at any time, with or without notice or cause. Nothing in this letter or XYZ's policies or procedures, either now or in the future, is intended to change the at-will nature of our relationship. No supervisor or other representative of the company has the authority to enter into any employment agreement that would be contrary to this employment at-will policy. Employees covered by a collective bargaining agreement should refer to the agreement for details on this subject.

Including a notice at the start of the employment relationship, declaring that it can be terminated at any time with or without cause, is a good first step toward setting proper expectations and possibly protecting the company from liability in the future.

The Resources

The Website *www.loc.gov/rr/news/stategov/stategov.html* provides helpful links to all official state homepages.

Workplace Fairness *www.workplacefairness.org/atwill.html* is a non-profit organization that helps to preserve and promote employee rights.

Inc.com has a sample at-will employment agreement on its Website at *www.inc.com/tools/2000/12/21528.html*.

The Website *www.willyancey.com/emp_law.htm*, compiled by Dr. Will Yancey, PhD, CPA, is a clearinghouse for a wealth of employment and benefits law Website links.

About.com has a fine summary of the federal laws that limit employment-at-will. Visit *http://jobsearchtech.about.com/od/careereducation/l/aa092402_3.htm*.

31

Written, Oral &
Implied Contracts

Defining Employment Contracts

Employment contracts come in many different forms, but generally fall into
three types:

1. Written

   Employees may be required to sign a standard written contract, or one
   that is applicable to his or her employment agreement.

2. Oral

   The employer and employee may have an oral agreement regarding the
   kind of work the employee will do, for how long, and at what rate of pay.

3. Implied

   Neither a written nor an oral agreement, but an implied contract based
   on the behavior of the employer.

While the differences may seem obvious especially for written and oral contracts,
an implied contract is more difficult to define and you may unknowingly give
employees a mixed signal that leads to misunderstandings and possible legal
action. This chapter covers the differences between these three types of contracts
and how each can be used effectively.

Written Contracts

The opposite of an oral contract is a written contract. Employers often believe
that having a contract with an employee automatically eliminates the freedom of
at-will status, but this is incorrect. When you hire someone at-will, you can fire the
employee for any or no reason at any time. Most states are at-will states. Absent a
contract stating otherwise, all employees are at-will employees and employers can
fire them for any or no reason at all, provided the termination does not constitute
illegal discrimination. A written contract defines the term of the employment
period, which makes the arrangement predictable for both parties, but it can
include an at-will clause.

Both the employee and employer should look for these simple but very important terms in a contract:

- Duties and responsibilities

  Provide a general job description reserving the right to amend or add to the employee's duties.

- Benefits

  Make clear that benefits such as health plans, bonuses, vacation time, memberships and car allowances are discretionary and may change at any time.

- Compensation

  Include salary, bonus, stock, retirement funds and signing bonus information.

- Term

  The contract need not be for a defined term but may include a guarantee of employee for a specified length of time.

- Relocation expenses

  Address how the employee will be reimbursed for relocation expenses.

- Expense accounts

  Define the type of out-of-pocket expenses that will be reimbursed.

- Termination clauses

  Describes in what circumstances either party can terminate the employment relationship.

- Non-compete clause

  An agreement that bars an employee from competing with a former employer–typically by working for a competing employer–for a certain period of time after employment ends.

- Choice of law

  Include a clause stating which jurisdiction the law will govern the contract.

- Attorney's fees

  Stipulate that if the employee brings suit against the company, the employee will pay the company's legal fees.

- Signatures

  The contract should be signed by both the company and the employee.

An employment contract need not be a long, difficult document, and it can be tailored for any employee. Employment contracts are not just for executives, though an employment contract for an executive will be more complex and detailed than for a staff employee or a middle manager. A well-written employment contract will settle disputes regarding employment. At the first sign of a dispute, the parties can look to the contract to confirm each side's rights and responsibilities. A good contract protects promises made by both parties.

Oral Contracts

Generally, oral contracts are just as enforceable as written contracts; however, contracts for a period of 1 year or more are only valid if in writing. The downside of an oral contract is that it is difficult to prove its existence if one side denies making the contract or disagrees with its terms. If an employment contract does not specify a period of time, the terms of the employee's employment can change at any time. For example, if an employee began work making $10 per hour, the rate could later be reduced to $9.50 per hour, as long as you provide the employee with written notice before the pay cut is instituted. Once you tell the employee that the wage is $9.50 and the employee continues to work, you most likely have just entered into a new contract with the employee for $9.50 per hour.

Supervisors, managers and administrators can sometimes unintentionally create a verbal contract with an employee by making statements that lead an employee to believe that there is a commitment by the company to employ him or her indefinitely. Examples of verbal statements to avoid include:

- Telling the employee that they do not need to worry about losing their job as long as they continue to do good work;
- telling an employee that the company never fires anyone; and
- describing a position as being a job for life.

You increase the likelihood that a verbal commitment will be viewed as a contract by the courts if an official action is taken that is consistent with the verbal commitment (e.g., the company president promises a job for life to a particular job candidate, and the Board then votes to approve the hiring of that job candidate). This action indicates an implied and oral contract.

One caveat is that if an employee believes your company has breached an oral contract, the burden of proof is on the employee to provide proof of the oral contract. The employee must produce substantial proof of an oral commitment in order to win a lawsuit.

Implied Contracts

Implied contracts are more common than written contracts in an employment relationship. They are often referred to as oral or implied contracts because they are created when an employer implies that a contract exists by means of a verbal statement. Thirty-eight states recognize an implied contract as an exception to at-will employment. Under the implied contract exception, you may not fire an employee when an implied contract is formed between an employer and employee, even though no express, written instrument regarding the employment relationship exists.

Good cause is key to an implied contract. An agreement that you, the employer will not fire the employee without good cause is the basic context of the implied contract in an employment relationship. You break an implied contract if:

- The implied contract said no termination without good cause;
- there was no good cause to fire the employee; or
- the employee was fired anyway.

A number of factors come into play in creating an implied contract:

- Length of service

  This is the most important element in creating an implied contract. Short-term employment does not create an implied contract, but generally involves years of service.

- Progressive discipline policy

  This type of policy states that an employee will not be fired for his or her first minor mistake; rather, you may issue a sequence of warnings before an employee is terminated.

- Employee benefit programs

  Benefits such as retirement programs, 401(k) programs, cafeteria plans and the like help to create implied employment contracts, because benefits imply that the employee expects to be around long enough to participate and receive benefits.

How do you avoid creating an implied contract inadvertently? The following suggestions will help you avoid creating an implied employment contract with an employee:

- Do not exaggerate during an interview. Do not promise the prospective employee that the only reason for termination is if he or she does the job poorly. Similarly, do not promise an automatic pay raise each year. Stress that the job requires a certain amount of flexibility to perform assigned duties and responsibilities.

- Include in the offer letter a confirmation of the offer, the starting date of employment, and explain that the employment relationship is at-will. Also include a definition of employment at-will for clarification.

- State compensation in terms of payroll payments rather than a yearly salary; such a statement could be misconstrued as a promise of at least a full year's employment and may be interpreted to be a contract.

- Identify contingencies of the offer, such as execution of a nondisclosure agreement. State that continued employment is conditional upon a number of factors, including but not limited to job performance and compliance with company policies and procedures.

- Never require a new hire to sign the offer letter, as it may be viewed as a written contract.

- Be cautious when issuing a raise, bonus or promotion. Avoid statements regarding longevity with the company, superior performance or essential skills.

- Your employee handbook should outline policies such as vacations, paid holidays, overtime and sick leave. Your handbook should also include an at-will disclaimer.

The Resources

Attorney David Greenberg explains the difference between implied and oral contracts at *www.discriminationattorney.com/oral_imp_cont.shtml#int_link_1*.

Free employment law advice is available at: *http://employment-law.freeadvice.com/hiring/implied_contracts.htm*.

Findlaw.com has an informative article at: *http://library.findlaw.com/2005/Mar/2/157726.html* entitled *Avoiding An Implied Employment Contract Or Drafting A Favorable One: A Prime*r by Nancy A. Newark.

32

Company Sponsored Events

Motivate and Thank Employees with Company Sponsored Events

As an owner or manager of a company, you look to provide every opportunity to motivate and thank employees for their hard work, dedication and responsibility. Employees are typically motivated by a number of factors: a steady paycheck; annual salary increases; a workplace free from tensions, bitterness and backbiting; the possibility of promotion; and an opportunity to build personal and professional skills.

Many employees will report that the little extras, when times are good, are especially appreciated: extra personal time, public recognition of a job well done, off-site seminars, and company sponsored events. Many managers encourage employees to interact outside of the office environment; this allows everyone, including managers, to see their co-workers in a different light, learn more about their interests, and meet their families. Employees often find that talking to the boss in an informal environment is a refreshing change from the daily grind.

Reasons that business owners commonly hold company sponsored events include:

- To thank employees for their work;
- to reward employees for reaching a specific goal; for example, by exceeding last year's sales;
- to enhance team building;
- to improve employee morale;
- to share in the financial success of the enterprise;
- to inform or educate employees about the organization in an informal way;
- to motivate employees to participate in community service; and
- to foster personal and professional growth among your employees

As a manager, you need to be clear as to your reasons for the outing. If your goal is for your employees to enjoy themselves at the company's expense, say so. Smaller companies may not have the financial resources to offer year-end bonuses, the use of company cars, or other more sophisticated rewards. Those same companies, however, may be able to order in pizza once a month.

Good Intentions Gone Wrong

What may seem like a generous, thoughtful plan to you might not be as well received by your employees, who may view it as an imposition. Take some time to plan the event. Survey your employees to learn their level of interest in various kinds of events. You may also suggest that employees volunteer to help plan the event. Popular activities include:

- a company-sponsored lunch monthly or quarterly
- an end-of-the-year dinner or banquet
- a group outing to a sporting event
- a company picnic
- a company sponsored softball game or golf outing
- a concert or theatre night
- a wine tasting

The list goes on and on. What is critical is that the events you sponsor have the effect you desire. One company had a standing committee whose goal was to organize at least one event a quarter, with all expenses paid by the company. A variety of activities were planned, including a ball game, an outdoor concert, and a museum tour.

Some sensitivity is needed to ensure that employees will not be goaded into doing something they do not want to do. If most of your employees live in the suburbs and commute to the city center for work, then a weekday dinner outing at a downtown restaurant may not be realistic or reasonable. Not everyone wants to play softball; older employees or those with disabilities may feel embarrassed or alienated.

Employees can interpret events that are held strictly for business purposes as work, rather than a social occasion (e.g., to formally recognize and impress shareholders or other stakeholders, bankers, vendors and others). A nice meal does not necessarily make up for the fact that employees have to return to work for a formal business event.

How Should People Behave

Some company sponsored parties have unexpectedly turned into absolute disasters of the first order. Everyone has witnessed the proverbial intoxicated employee wearing the lamp shade; loud, boorish, confrontational, and uninhibited. It is important to establish ground rules to avoid this embarrassing behavior.

First, be honest about the nature of the event. If the event is truly work related, be sure to communicate this to your employees. Do not pretend that the party is designed as a purely social occasion. If spouses are expected to attend, explain why; but understand that some spouses may have valid reasons for not attending. For formal events such as this, you should distribute a memo indicating the reason for the occasion, proper dress for the evening, and what is expected of employees. Explain the importance of your employees' behavior at the event; make it clear that the entire company needs to make a strong, positive impression. If the event occurs on a work night, allow employees to leave a bit early so that they may return properly dressed.

Second, if the event is purely a social one, explain this to everyone so that they know that it is to be fun and a reward for a job well done. No one wants to be told that they should build morale; if that is your motivation, choose instead to invite speakers and consultants in during working hours.

Set the agenda clearly. Indicate whether the event is informal, whether spouses and friends are invited, and set reasonable rules, such as limiting or eliminating alcohol. It is particularly important that you politely explain to employees and supervisors that this is not the time to have an out-of-office discussion about differences of opinion, or in any way use the occasion to be confrontational.

Company-sponsored events need not be elaborate or expensive to be appreciated. One small company organized a bimonthly event called Lunch and Learn, at which a buffet lunch was served. Different people chose the menu each time, and were sensitive to individual tastes and preferences (e.g., for vegetarian items). An educational or informational segment was attached to each lunch–presentations on sales, profitability to date, plans for growth, team progress, and so forth. On occasion, a speaker was invited to talk about something other than business– financial or retirement planning, additions to company benefits, introducing new employees, cultural events, and more.

The Resources

The Website *www.2006-deals.com* serves as an Internet clearing house that can assist you in planning company sponsored events. You can find everything from the International Speakers Bureau (ISB) to organizations that will plan and book your event for you.

Performance Appraisal

The First Challenge

How to Make Your Employees See the Advantages of Performance Appraisal

Many employees tune out when they hear the term performance appraisal. All too often, employees view the performance appraisal process as stressful, negative, or even a waste of time. Employees tend to see only the negative aspects of performance appraisal. Some may feel that the process is only there to help the company weed out bad employees. This perspective comes from the time when almost all performance appraisals were of the traditional type, and more a judgment on the employee's performance than a tool for developing better employees. Traditional performance appraisals are one-sided and give the employee little opportunity to participate. While some companies still employ the traditional kind of assessment process, current trends favor a more developmental approach where the employee is given tools for improvement.

It is not only employees who balk at the performance appraisal process. Supervisors do not always buy into it either. They frequently see a formal performance appraisal process as wasted paperwork and worry that it will interfere with their preferred coaching style. Other concerns voiced by managers include their own inability to give feedback, the employee's capacity to receive feedback, and the fact that the process may show deficiencies in their own performance that they prefer to hide. They make excuses for not evaluating their employees by claiming that everyone is much too busy or that the time just is not right.

These fears demonstrate why performance appraisal–and its corollaries, peer reviews and self-evaluation–often receives an undeserved bad rap. One of your goals as an employer is to train all your employees, management and non-management, to use the performance appraisal process to better their job performance and strengthen their life skills. One of the best strategies for ensuring your employees participate in the process is to tie annual increases with performance appraisals. Doing this will almost ensure 100 percent participation by both management and staff.

Getting everyone on board needs to be a top priority if you want to reap the benefits from this process. All employees need to be involved in the process at some level. This is important for consistency, but also because all employees can profit from the experience. Employees need to know that having their performance assessed regularly improves their working experience. They need to be made to understand that a part of assessing performance is evaluating the supervisor and the training the employee is receiving. It also includes appraising the working conditions. It is not just about judging the employee. Done correctly, it is an opportunity to see what is working and what needs to be improved, both on the non-management and management levels. The direct advantage to the employee is that receiving feedback consistently and increasing supervisor and employee communication allows employees to know what is expected of them. Having a clear idea of expectations and standards enables employees to focus better and enhances their performance. This in turn increases the employee's self-esteem and builds morale throughout the department. It will also enable you to recognize high performers, which is beneficial since all employees, no matter what their level, want to be recognized and appreciated.

There are other benefits to creating and developing a performance appraisals system. Companies using a consistent performance appraisal system often discover the following:

- Improved Communication
    - Employees and the supervising staff learn skills that enable them to communicate effectively with each other. They are also given the time to focus on this and understand that it is a company priority.
    - Employees learn how to communicate among themselves. They also realize that there is a process in place to address problems.

- Clearer Definition of Individual Goals
    - Most employees perform their jobs with long-range goals. Many people expect to be promoted or change jobs to improve their economic and social status within the company. The job performance process enables them to participate in a process that clarifies their expectations and helps them reach their own goals.

- Clearer Definition of Company Goals
    - The way you develop and administer your own performance appraisal program provides insight into the company's goals and mission. By highlighting concerns and areas that are important to you, you can also

make sure that your employees' goals are aligned with yours.

- Improved Employee Performance
  - By requiring employees to analyze their day-to-day performance, you have an opportunity to discover what each job actually entails. Since most jobs change over time, you should take advantage of the information supplied and make sure your job descriptions actually reflect the work required.
  - You can see in which areas your employees need improvement and provide the proper training and procedures necessary for correcting the deficiencies. You will also see which employees may not work out and begin the proper process ending your employment relationship with them.
  - By providing strategies to rectify difficult situations, you are giving the manager critical assistance. A staff that is assisted and supported performs better.
  - Employees who feel that they are doing well are less likely to leave your company. Fewer turnovers means less money spent in recruiting and training new employees.

Companies frequently find that acclimating employees to the concept of performance appraisals and self-assessments early in the employment relationship works best. When an employee knows that the first assessment will be at the 3-month point, he or she will approach their training and performance with a sense of purpose. The direction that this can provide is invaluable as it can set the tone for the days to come.

Once you have made the decision to implement a performance appraisal process, there are many points that you need to consider.

- Are you going to use a pre-packaged system or develop your own?
- How often will each employee be reviewed?
- Will you have a probationary period?
- Will your process include peer reviews?
- Will your process include self-assessment?
- Will the employee's manager review the results or will that fall to human resources? You can also use outside firms to create and run your performance appraisal program.

No matter which system you choose, your employees should be setting goals. A highly recommended method for writing goals is the SMART system; the acronym stands for specific, measurable, attainable, realistic and tangible. Your human resources staff and the employee's manager need to work with the employee to make sure that they have SMART goals and logical action plans in place to meet those goals. The more you and your employees put into the process, the more everyone will benefit.

The Second Challenge

How to Use Performance Appraisal to Weed Out Unsuccessful Employees

The performance appraisal performance is equally critical in cases where employees simply do not work out. If your employees have been faithfully participating in the process, and your managers are honest with you, you will be aware of possible problem employees. While a primary purpose of performance evaluation is to make good employees better, evaluations also tell you early on which employees are just not a good fit for your company. When you see documented evidence that a particular employee does not meet expectations or needs improvement in multiple areas, it is time to take serious action. Within the process, there are many disciplinary components at your disposal. Verbal and written warnings are a good beginning. You can also place an employee on a performance improvement plan. Working with difficult employees may be unpleasant, but it is a necessary part of business. These steps must be taken to ensure that termination is the correct action and that you are rightfully terminating the employee.

By regularly reviewing your employees and documenting their performance, you will have the necessary information to end the employee-employer relationship without risking litigation. Your former employee will have no basis to sue if you use a strong, participatory performance appraisal and document that you have worked with the employee every step of the way. If you can demonstrate that the expectations were clear from the start and that the proper training and employee support was provided, the termination will stick and you will be able to close the books on an employee who just did not work out.

The Resources

Many Websites are available to guide you in developing your own performance appraisal system. These include *www.hronline.com*, *http://performance-appraisals.org* and *www.blr.com*.

Other Websites mentioned in previous chapters that also contain information on performance appraisal systems include *www.toolkit.cch.com* and *www.allbusiness.com*.

Companies such as Hewitt, PeopleSoft and Parthenon Group specialize in human resources. If you choose to outsource your performance management system needs, they can tailor a system specific to your company's needs.

Progressive Discipline

Creating and Enforcing Proper Disciplinary Procedures

Telling an employee that he or she is not doing well–or worse–is a difficult task for any manager or owner. Criticism stings no matter how kindly it is given. Unfortunately, poor employee performance rarely improves on its own. If it is left unchecked, you may fire the employee in a fit of anger and risk a wrongful termination lawsuit. As a person with a leadership role in the company, you must take action to correct substandard performance.

Consciously or unconsciously, most companies accomplish this through progressive discipline. Progressive discipline is a behavior modification approach that entails changing unacceptable employee conduct through a step-by-step program of increasing negative consequences. These consequences are usually determined by the type of infraction or improper behavior and the employee's past record. The penalties that typically comprise progressive discipline programs can run the gamut from simple verbal warnings and admonishments to terminations. Obviously, your goal in most cases is to modify the behavior so that you do not have to fire the employee.

Progressive discipline is not for those rare instances where the first offense is so egregious that you have no recourse; you must fire the employee. Examples of these types of cases are theft, destruction of property, intoxication on the job, sexual harassment, assault and fraud. Nonetheless, you should not fire the employee on the spot, but rather take the time to investigate. Firing is a very serious action and you want to make sure that you have all the facts. You do not want to give the employee any cause to bring legal action against you.

Fortunately, most employee problems usually involve poor performance, not criminal conduct. Many performance issues can be solved with the manager or with some targeted coaching. When these casual remedies are unsuccessful, either because the employee continues to perform poorly or ignore the rules, it is time to apply your progressive discipline program. It is with these cases that progressive discipline is practiced often quite successfully. The key is to make sure that you and your managers are vigilant at catching performance issues when they occur so that you increase your chances at successfully modifying the behavior.

There are many advantages to establishing a written disciplinary procedure:

- Creating the policy in advance of any adverse circumstances helps ensure that your policy will not be based upon emotion. It will be a rational policy, carefully listing the type of the infraction and the logical consequence for that behavior. A written policy gives you the ability to enumerate all the potential problems and how you plan to address them.
- Having a formal written policy ensures that you and your employees are all on the same page. Placing the policy within your employee manual and having the employee sign off on it should help prevent miscommunications and misunderstandings that can lead to legal action against you.
- A progressive discipline policy allows correcting only the behavior of those employees that need it. In other words, you do not need to take away telephone privileges of an entire department or floor just because one employee is flagrantly violating the rules by receiving too many personal calls. You can simply discipline only that employee.
- Having and following a progressive discipline policy provides protection against legal action.

This is not to say that there are no downsides to progressive discipline. Some of the problems include:

- A progressive discipline policy requires a great deal of documentation. It is usually a very intricate process with many steps and requires significant paperwork. The amount of paperwork involved could make it impossible for some very small businesses to handle, and so they may decide that it is not worth the time.
- Both management and non-management employees need to be trained on the policy. It needs to be explained clearly so that there is no danger of miscommunication or misinterpretation.
- Once written, a progressive discipline policy must be followed, so you have to ensure that you and your managers enforce it. Both management and non-management employees need to understand that the written policy is the only policy.
- A progressive discipline policy does not always adequately address basic incompetence or poor employee-job fit.

While these disadvantages do not outweigh the advantages, they need to be considered when a company is deciding whether to implement a progressive discipline policy.

So what are the key components to a progressive discipline system?

- Both the employee and employer are aware at the outset of the specific consequences for breaking an employee rule.
- Each occurrence of the same violation is treated the same unless there are mitigating or aggravating conditions.
- The poor performance issues and the violations of company policy must be clearly defined.
- The severity of the punishment increases for repeated occurrences within a certain time period.
- The severity of the punishment is dependent upon the infraction.
- The disciplinary action must be enforceable.

When setting up your own disciplinary policy, you need to consider the structure of your employment manual. The progressive disciplinary program is a part of your employee manual. As such, it should be formatted in the same way, both for clarity and to demonstrate that it is an integral part of your employee policies and procedures. Unfortunately, you cannot sugarcoat employee job violations or poor performance and their consequences. You must clarify your position from the very beginning.

What your policy should contain:

1. Definition of infractions. These should include:
   a. Attendance issues
      i. Absenteeism
      ii. Tardiness
      iii. Shorting the company hours
      iv. Abuse of sick leave, personal or vacation days
   b. Behavior issues
      i. Insubordination, both one-time instances and chronic
      ii. Failure to get along with co-workers and teammates
      iii. Dress code violations
   c. Electronic communication devices policies
      i. Excessive personal calls
      ii. Excessive personal usage of the Internet and e-mail
      iii. Inappropriate usage of the telephone, Internet or e-mail
   d. Illegal conduct
      i. Drug, alcohol and weapons on the premises
      ii. Inappropriate sexual, religious, ethnic or gender discrimination or harassment

e. Poor performance
    i. Multiple instances over specified time of failure to meet standards or needs improvement
    ii. Comprehension issues; the employee's inability to *get it*
    iii. Consistent mistakes; failure to perform job efficiently and effectively

2. Definition of disciplinary actions based upon type of violation and length of time between infractions
    a. Verbal warning
    b. Written warning
    c. Placement of individual on personal improvement plan
    d. Suspension
    e. Termination

Personal improvement plans (PIPs) can be initiated either after rule and policy violations or in response to poor performance documented in an employee's routine performance appraisals. While some employees may view such a plan as the beginning of the end, PIPs can often make a difference if they are taken seriously and executed properly.

If you are clear as to your company's policies and the consequences for violating them, you will have more success in developing employees that you want to retain. You will spend less time reinventing the wheel and arguing with your employees because these policies will be in place. It is important to remember that a progressive disciplinary policy is one more piece in your employee management arsenal, and goes hand-in-hand with performance appraisals and your employee manual. You can maximize your employees' performance by using all of these tools.

Do not forget to document all incidents, regardless of the type of problem or offense. Even a verbal warning must be documented and placed in the manager's file. Assuming you have played by the rules, a paper trail that includes an enforceable and enforced progressive disciplinary policy will be crucial in a successful defense of a wrongful termination charge.

The Resources

These Websites address human resource concerns such as progressive discipline: *www.humanresources.about.com*, *www.allbusiness.com* and *www.citehr.com*.

Documentation

Having the Right Documents to Prevent Termination Lawsuits

When an employee hears the good news, you are hired, that message is almost always given and received in good faith. Both the employee and the company believe that this step is in the best interest of both parties and so goodwill abounds. Unfortunately, this does not always turn out to be the case. For whatever reasons, not all employer-employee relationships end well. In some cases, the employee resigns on his or her own, and in other instances, the employee is terminated. So even though most employers do not hire someone with the intention of eventually firing them, employers need to be prepared.

In order to reduce your anxiety when you have to terminate an employee, you need to make sure you have procedures in place that document employee problems as they occur. This means that you should have a formalized structure and procedure that documents your rules and policies. If you have followed all the traditional rules for managing your company well, you have an employee manual, a performance appraisal system, and steps for progressive discipline all in place, ready to be used. The development of these tools has taught your organization how to be prepared for all situations; the trick is to make sure your managers use them properly.

Therein lies the rub. It is all well and good to have these systems in place, but they must be utilized to be effective and to provide any protection for you at all. These documents have a twofold purpose: to develop effective, productive employees and to terminate when appropriate. Your rules and policies must be applied consistently to all your employees; the inclination to treat problems on a case-by-case basis or by intuition must be suppressed. You have spent considerable amounts of time and money to develop these documents, and you need to make sure that you also spend the appropriate amount of time to train your managers in their usage. By using the procedures you have in place to document performance problems and achievements, you can prevent serious legal problems later. This actually safeguards both you and your employees and is in everyone's best interest.

Train your managers to keep records. Make it clear to them that they must document all incidents and take copious notes. They need to understand that keeping a paper trail is not just important, it is critical. No one can remember every little detail. Events and time sequences get mixed up and are not reliable. Most importantly, actual paper documents are much more convincing than someone's word in a court of law. You must develop an enforceable strategy to make sure your managers put everything in writing. Remember, they are your employees and are therefore accountable to you.

You also will need to be upfront with your non-management employees. They should know at the outset that your company is professional and expects its employees to behave the same. The employee manual that you give them and that they acknowledge will have your disciplinary procedures and other policies outlined clearly. The employees will see that if they are on the receiving end of corrective action, each stage will be documented carefully and put into their file.

There are those companies that prefer a more casual approach to documentation. Management believes in writing everything down but does not take the time to fill out specific forms created for this purpose. This is not the recommended route, because there is too great a tendency to write the minimum and leave out pertinent information. While jotting down notes is an integral part of the documentation process, it cannot be the entire process.

A much safer method is to use preprinted forms that ask specific questions. The form should be a fill-in-the-blank format that enables the manager to provide the relevant information plus ample room for comments and examples. Blanks to be filled in should include:

- Name and position of employee
- Name and position of supervisor
- Current date
- Date infraction or event occurred
- Details of event
- Rule or policy violated
- Employee's reaction
- Whether this is the first, second or third offense
- Action taken
- Place for employee signature
- Place for employee comments (if desired)

You cannot play games. The employee must know that this behavior or incident will be added to his or her permanent record. That is why it is essential that the employee see and sign the disciplinary form. He or she also must understand that there will be consequences, which must be spelled out in no uncertain terms.

In addition to doing the necessary paperwork for a serious infraction, managers should become accustomed to keeping records informally. This includes writing notes (both positive and negative) in employees' files, printing and saving important e-mails, and generally noting any event or conversation that could prove useful in defending a wrongful termination accusation. These seemingly little things can play a huge role if you are ever sued.

This philosophy needs to be driven home to your managers. Most managers find it quite distasteful to tell an employee that they are doing poorly or have violated a company rule or policy. It is human nature to shy away from conflicts or look the other way. As a general rule people want to be liked, and so they avoid doing something that will anger someone else. Requiring your managers to write notes when something troublesome occurs will give them the ammunition to confront the hard stuff. If they get into the habit of jotting down notes from a conversation or printing a particularly inappropriate e-mail, they will find it easier to move to the next step when necessary. While you do not want your manager to become obsessed with notetaking, the reality is that there can never be too much documentation.

The notes must be specific. They must state the situation and what the employee did incorrectly. Providing concrete examples is crucial. The manager cannot rely on feelings or beliefs, but must state the problem accurately. For example, it is not enough to write that the employee was insubordinate; the employee's statements and actions should be documented as explicitly as possible. If you and your managers become vigilant at writing notes, keeping records and doing the necessary paperwork, you will find that it will become part of the daily routine. Once written, the notes should be placed in the manager's file for the employee. This way they can either be used later or discarded if the problems are resolved or the employee leaves of his or her own accord.

How long to keep this information is another important consideration. Most companies keep all employee records for the duration of employment, and often for a year or two afterwards—even longer if the employee was terminated. Some organizations, on the other hand, cull their files after 5 to 10 years or even earlier. If you believe that there is the faintest chance you will need this evidence, it should be kept permanently, even after the employee no longer works for you. If the employee has rectified the improper behavior, you may choose to remove the record after a year. Ultimately, the choice is up to you.

The importance of keeping excellent records and documenting cannot be stressed enough. You never want to take action against an employee without having your facts documented. Having the hard evidence to back up your allegations gives you the confidence to do the right thing and the ability to defend your position. Do not let your managers take the easy way out, but train them how to document and make sure that they do.

The Resources

These Websites have a variety of human resource forms available for purchase: *www.smallbizresource.com*, *www.hrpolicyanswers.com*, and *www.alllaw.com*.

Other general references include *The American Bar Association Guide to Workplace Law: Everything You Need to Know About Your Rights as an Employee or Employer* at *www.hr-guide.com*.

Plant Closing– Union Rules/State Laws

Eliminating Jobs and Assisting Dislocated Employees

In 2005 the Bureau of Labor Statistics reported on 1,183 plant and distribution center closures, partial closures and relocations, dislocating 15,699 workers. This number is up slightly over 2004 figures. In our changing economy, many companies continue to streamline their operations to maintain a competitive foothold in the marketplace. Although such actions can help your company become more efficient, it also means you may be forced to eliminate existing jobs and facilities. There are a number of rules and regulations you must follow to comply with federal and state guidelines.

Smaller companies can simply close, lock the doors and walk away. However, there are circumstances that trigger the WARN act and you must provide employees advance notification of the closing. See Chapter 42 for details.

Getting Help

If you are closing a plant or laying off workers within an operating unit, the Department of Labor offers programs to assist you and your displaced employees. The programs are called Rapid Response Service and Trade Adjustment Assistance and Alternative Trade Adjustment Assistance. The benefits to you and your employees are outlined below along with key contact information and additional resources.

Rapid Response Service

Recognizing that in this highly competitive, global marketplace companies are constantly growing and shrinking to remain competitive, the Department of Labor has created a service called Rapid Response Service made up of state and local resources that can assist your company and employees during a mass layoff or plant closing. The Rapid Response teams work with employers and any employee representative to maximize quickly public and private resources to minimize the disruptions on companies, affected workers and communities that are associated with job loss.

The more quickly the Rapid Response strategy is implemented, the better off your company and workers will be. Contact your state's Dislocated Worker Unit, *http://www.doleta.gov/layoff/rapid_coord.cfm,* by notifying them of impending layoffs.

Trade Adjustment Assistance (TAA) & Alternative Trade Adjustment Assistance (ATAA)

The federal government provides additional services to workers whose jobs are lost due to foreign trade or shifts in production out of the United States. While not all job loss due to foreign competition meets the requirements of the Trade Act, the Rapid Response team will work with your company to provide information on TAA and the benefits you can receive if your company is certified as trade-affected. Your company, the Rapid Response team, or the workers themselves can file a trade petition with the United States Department of Labor.

Training is provided to certified workers who do not have the skills to secure suitable employment in the existing labor market. Training is targeted to a specific occupation and provided to help certified workers secure employment at a skill level similar to or higher than their layoff employment, and sustain that employment at the best wage available. Based on the individual's existing skills and labor market conditions, training will be of the shortest duration necessary to return the individual to employment.

Trade Readjustment Allowances (TRA)

Provides income support to displaced workers while they are participating in full-time training. Under certain circumstances TRA is also available to certified workers for whom training is not feasible or appropriate.

Each category has its own set of eligibility requirements. Visit the Department of Labor at *http://www.doleta.gov/tradeact/* to learn more about qualifications and benefits.

TAA Program Services and Benefits

TAA program benefits and services are provided to help eligible workers get back to work. Certified workers who apply for TAA services and benefits may be eligible for the following:

Rapid Response Assistance

Provided by the Dislocated Worker Unit in the state where workers are laid off. Rapid Response assistance is provided to every group of workers on whose behalf a petition is filed. Rapid Response staff will make employees aware of the different services available to workers after a layoff is announced.

Employment Services

Offer workers assistance in finding a new job. Many TAA-eligible workers will be able to return to employment through a combination of these services. For individuals who require retraining, these services will help identify appropriate training programs, and help them obtain reemployment at the conclusion of the training program.

Job Search Allowances

May be payable to cover expenses incurred in seeking employment outside a certified worker's normal commuting area, if a suitable job is not available in the area. Job search allowances reimburse 90 percent of the total costs of allowable travel and subsistence, up to a total of $1,250.

Training

Is provided to certified workers who do not have the skills to secure suitable employment in the existing labor market. Training is targeted to a specific occupation and provided to help certified workers secure employment at a skill level similar to or higher than their layoff employment, and sustain that employment at the best wage available.

Your state may offer incumbent worker training programs to help upgrade your workers' skills, employer loan programs, and other services that may help avert or minimize layoffs. The Rapid Response team can provide information on these programs. Here are some links to organizations and resources that might be beneficial to your company:

Your State Division of Economic Development office helps existing businesses expand and assists local development efforts.

The Resources

www.dol.gov/compliance/guide/layoffs.htm

> State Rapid Response Center Coordinators are listed in alphabetical order, including the department address, phone number and email address of the state contact.

www.dol.gov/elaws/

The elaws Advisors are interactive e-tools that provide easy-to-understand information about a number of federal employment laws. Each Advisor simulates the interaction you might have with an employment law expert. It asks questions and provides answers based on responses given. Both employees and employers can benefit from elaws. Choose from one of the topics listed to find an elaws Advisor of interest to you.

www.taacenters.org/locations.html

Trade Adjustment Assistance for Firms (TAA) is a federal program that provides financial assistance to manufacturers affected by import competition. Sponsored by the U.S. Department of Commerce, this federal assistance program helps pay for projects that improve a firm's competitiveness.

www.doleta.gov/layoff/pdf/EmployerWARN09_2003.pdf

Employer's Guide to Advance Notice of Closings and Layoffs. Worker Adjustment and Retraining Notification (WARN) Act.

www.bls.gov/mls/

Bureau of Labor Statistics Mass Layoff Statistics Website page.

www.servicelocator.org/

Workers can find the One-Stop Career Center closest to them by calling 877.US2.JOBS toll-free, 877.889.5627 (TTY).

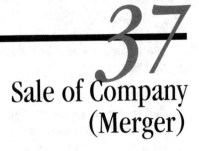

Sale of Company (Merger)

Striking the Right Balance

The sale of every business is unique. If your business has more than 100 workers, you will handle the sale differently than a company that has only 20 workers. How should workers be notified of the sale? When should I tell my employees about the sale? Is the buyer or seller responsible for notifying the employees? Should I ask employees to sign a non-disclosure statement or non-compete agreement? Will the business falter if too many employees jump to competitors? When selling your business, you not only have to worry about finding a buyer, but also about keeping your employees motivated and keeping company secrets from being disclosed. In this chapter we will review when is a good time to notify workers of the company's sale; the proper procedures to follow once the sale has been completed; and who is responsible for informing workers of a sale or takeover.

Notifying the Employees

In the sale of a business there is always an employer who is responsible for giving notice to the employees that the business has been sold. The next issue is when should the employees be told. Some experts believe it is best to tell employees about the sale immediately before or immediately after the sale is complete. If there are employees whose expertise will be needed after the sale, these employees should be introduced to the buyer shortly before closing.

Others believe that the employees should hear about a potential sale of the business from you and not from a third party. Rumors breed nervousness, and it is demoralizing to hear from an outside source that the company is up for sale. Some of your staff may worry about uncertainty and look for employment elsewhere before a new buyer can be found. If you choose to advertise the sale of your business openly, inform your employees before the advertisements run. Explain that the sale could take a long time to happen and–unless you plan to close down if no sale occurs–may not happen at all. You may even decide that one of your employees is the best potential buyer for your business. After all, your employees know the business best; they may be able to persuade investors or lending institutions to help finance a leveraged buyout, or at the very least help to find a buyer.

If you plan to find a buyer who will keep all or most of your employees on the payroll, communicate this with the staff. It is best to be truthful and emphasize the positive. If you decide to advertise the business confidentially, make a concerted effort to avoid any leaks to employees. Consider using the services of a business broker or have interested buyers sign a non-disclosure agreement. Arrange to show potential buyers around the company during off hours.

Completing the Sale

If you sell your business and the buyer decides to retain the existing employees, the purchaser is treated as a successor employer. A successor employer is defined as a new owner that acquires substantially all the property used in the trade or business and employs the individuals, who prior to the acquisition, were employed by the former owner (the predecessor employer). Unless there is an express agreement stating otherwise, the purchasing company will recognize prior employment service terms (the employee maintains all benefits and credit for past services to the company) of the existing employees for the purposes of termination and severance calculations. The new employer has an obligation to maintain pay equity plans already in place and to offer a competitive wage relative to its competitors.

If the business is sold without employees, the employees may have an option to enter into a new contract of employment (if there is an offer of employment) with the buyer and they do not receive credit for past service given to the company. If the new employer terminates employees after the sale then the buyer must comply with the termination and severance provisions as determined by the WARN Act.

Collective Agreements and the Union

If the company employs workers that are members of a trade union, the union and its collective agreements continue to be in force as long as there is a continuation of the same business. The new employer also inherits all existing proceedings such as grievance arbitration, discrimination suits or wage issues, and is expected to address any breaches of the collective bargaining agreement that may have been pending before the company was sold. Any grievances against the old employer now become the problem of the new employer.

In the event the new employer is already bound by a collective bargaining agreement with another union, if appropriate, the two unions may be combined into one. If one union is significantly smaller than the other, the agreement of the larger union will generally stay in force. If necessary, the union may conduct a member vote to choose by majority which union will represent them, and that union's agreement will be adopted.

Pension Plans

When a company is sold, pension plan assets may or may not be transferred to the new owner. The new employer has the option to:

- Terminate the old company's pension plan;
- invite inherited employees to participate in the new pension plan;
- replace mandatory participation in the pension plan for voluntary participation; or
- take over the old company's pension plan in its entirety.

Employees whose employment is terminated as a result of the sale may have their plans terminated as well. They may be given the option to receive the vested portion of their pension in a lump sum payout, or assets may be left in the old plan, with no further payouts or contributions from the new employer. For the employees who remain, the pension plan may be terminated if the new employer does not have in existence a pension plan for employees, or if the new employer does not want to assume the liability for the old employer's plan.

In the event the new employer does have an existing pension plan, the affected employees may be invited to join the plan. Depending on how the pension plan is set up, the assets from the old plan may or may not be transferred to the new plan.

A partial plan termination may occur if members move from a mandatory participation plan to a voluntary plan. Transferring members may be given a one-time option to opt out; those who do will no longer be a part of the plan.

Finally, the new employer may assume the pension plan from the old employer. This is possible only if the new employer takes over the entire business covered by the plan. Otherwise it will be considered a partial plan termination.

Hostile Takeover

What happens when there is a hostile takeover or forced sale of a company? Who is responsible for notifying employees of a plant closing or mass layoff? Each situation is different and can be handled differently.

In the event of a hostile takeover that does not include the employees, the buyer is responsible for providing notice of any covered plant closing or mass layoff that may occur after the sale. The obvious problem with this is that the buyer is not the employer at the time notice must be given; if the seller does not cooperate, the buyer may not know the names and addresses of everyone who will be affected so that it can give individual notice. Regardless, written notice is still required by the WARN Act.

If the sale of the company is without employees, and if the seller is aware of a definitive plan on the part of the buyer to close a plant or conduct mass layoffs, the seller becomes liable for sending out termination notices to employees notifying them of the plant closing or mass layoff that will be taking place after the date of the sale.

In the event the buyer retains the employees for a brief period after the sale, but then decides to terminate them within 60 days of the sale, the buyer is liable for the full 60-day notice, if applicable.

Constructive Discharge

If an employee turns down an offer of employment with the new employer, it is considered a voluntary departure unless the offer constitutes a constructive discharge. This can include situations in which significant changes are made in employee's wages, benefits, working conditions or job description. The same holds true if a drastic change in wages or working conditions causes a person to believe he or she was being fired or would be unable to continue working for that employer; this could constitute a constructive discharge. The test is usually a matter of state law and the test is often a strict one.

Selling a company can produce many different emotions. There are so many things to consider, but most importantly, how your employees will adapt to the new owners and working conditions. You can help bridge the gap by working cooperatively with the new owners to ensure your employees are treated fairly and receive ample notification of pending changes. It is your business and you have the power to make the transition smooth.

The Resources

The Website *www.allbusiness.com/business_advice/Advice_index.asp* contains expert advice for the small business owner on selling a business.

Nolo Press has a resource center on its Website devoted to selling a business, *www.nolo.com/resource.cfm/catID/C1DBB6FC-F9C3-40CA-8A4D77366ED0D4 D5/111/254/*.

Visit the About.com small business resource center for additional information: *http://sbinformation.about.com/od/buyingorselling/*.

Martindale-Hubbell offers legal advice on buying and selling a business at *www.lawyers.com/lawyers/P~B~Buying%20or%20Selling%20a%20Business~ LDS.html.*

When to Terminate

Knowing When to Fire an Employee

Hiring an employee may be complicated, but terminating an employee is far more difficult. It takes a great deal of time, effort and care to choose the best candidate from among many applicants. Firing an employee–a person with whom you have an established relationship–takes even more time, effort and care. It is critical to take this step slowly and make certain you are doing what is best for the company and what is appropriate under the law. The best safeguard against potential legal action is to consult with an attorney who specializes in employment law before you take any action.

Most employees in the United States are at-will employees. This means that unless there is a signed contract that indicates terms of employment, both the employer and the employee have the right to terminate the relationship at any time and for any reason. By no means does this give a manager or owner free rein to fire anyone without cause. It does, however, mean that there is a large amount of latitude when an employment relationship heads south. While most owners and managers would never consider using any of the following as grounds to fire someone, these conditions also need to be spelled out for human resource professionals to ensure that the law is not violated.

Illegal or Inappropriate Reasons to Terminate

- Employee reported on illegal or potentially illegal or immoral activity (whistleblowing). If the employee in question has made a claim or reported possible illegal activity to the EEOC, typically in the form of a discrimination claim, that employee is absolutely untouchable at least until the claim is resolved. These claims include: race, color, religion, national origin, sex, age or disability under federal law. If the employee has not lodged a formal complaint with the EEOC, but has complained to his or her supervisor or to human resources, firing him or her at this juncture is not recommended. Any action taken at this time would be viewed as retaliatory and would probably be grounds for a lawsuit. You also cannot fire the employee if he or she caught your company engaging in any illegal activity such as falsifying the books or covering up accidents.

- Employee is pregnant. If the employee you wish to terminate has announced that she is pregnant, you cannot fire her. Pregnancy is deemed a temporary disability and as such must be treated like all temporary disabilities. Both Title VII of the Civil Rights Act of 1964, which includes the Pregnancy Discrimination Act of 1978 and the Family and Medical Leave Act of 1993, cover pregnancies.
- Employee is under contract. While contracts can be broken, it is not a wise policy to fire an employee that is covered by an employment agreement unless he or she has first violated the contract.
- Employee has been promised job security or other terms of employment. If the employee was guaranteed job security or tenure, you cannot fire this employee without the risk of a lawsuit or other legal action.
- Employee was performing a public duty or obligation. If the employee missed work due to jury duty or exercising his or her right to vote, he or she cannot be terminated without the risk of a lawsuit or other legal action.

If there is any chance that your termination of a particular employee is for the wrong reasons, consult with your employment attorney. This cannot be stressed enough. The best protection you have is consulting with a professional that knows the law.

Once you have cleared these hurdles and are relatively confident that you will not be inviting obvious legal action by firing the specific employee, it is time to really examine your case.

Having a Business Case

While at-will employees can be dismissed at any time and for any reason, it is always better to have a business case to support your decision. The importance of an employee manual cannot be overemphasized. Every business needs to have an employee manual that delineates the company's policies and procedures. The manual must contain clearly written policies for termination and the company must follow them. Each employee should sign a document indicating that they have read these policies and understand them.

A final check in ascertaining whether the termination is the correct step is to consider whether a neutral third party would consider termination the reasonable response to the behavior. If you are confident that firing the employee in question is the only logical action and that others outside the company would see it the same way, then you can and should proceed.

Legal and Appropriate Reasons to Terminate

- **Employee is discovered conducting illegal activities.** If an employee is caught stealing, possessing or using drugs, or physically assaulting another employee in clear violation of the law, termination is in order. In some instances, even threatening a fellow employee with physical violence may be enough to terminate. Make sure that you have proof of any of these activities before you take this step.

- **Employee has committed sexual harassment.** It should go without saying that warnings against committing sexual harassment should be in your employment manual. Sexual harassment is not only harmful to a good working environment; it is also illegal. All employees should know that committing sexual harassment is grounds for termination. Therefore, if you have proof that this offense has occurred, termination of the offending employee is the proper step.

- **Employee is in a supervisory position and has discriminated against subordinates in terms of race, color, religion, national origin, sex, age or disability.** These behaviors violate federal law and are also automatic grounds for dismissal.

- **Employee has been performing poorly.** If you have decided that an employee does not meet the minimum standards for employment, it is time to let this employee go. It is critical to have accurate, timely documentation to back up your decision. You have to make certain that the employee was evaluated based upon company standards just like every other employee and that his or her supervisor documented the problems. Moreover, if this employee had recently received a favorable review, your standing to fire this employee becomes considerably shakier. You need to make sure that the action matches the behavior. Before the extreme action of firing is taken, consider whether putting the employee on a performance improvement plan first might be the better course of action.

- **Employee has been chronically tardy and/or demonstrated excessive absenteeism.** Again, the key is documentation. You cannot even begin to contemplate taking this course of action unless you can empirically prove the unacceptable behavior. Another thing to remember is this action this will be much easier to take if this undesirable behavior is listed in the employee manual as grounds for termination.

- **Employee spends excessive time on the telephone making personal calls, surfing the Internet, chatting with co-workers, taking prolonged lunches or breaks.** These behaviors are absolutely causes for termination, but must be documented. There must be concrete examples of the behavior to make the case and prevent any course of legal action by the terminated employee.

You also must be certain that you are treating all employees equally and enforcing the rules for everyone.

- Employee has given away trade secrets or inside information. If the employee has been privy to sensitive information and has shared it outside the company or inappropriately within the company and has been warned, your logical recourse would be to terminate him or her.

No matter what the reason an employee is to be terminated, it is imperative to remember the following:

- Document, document, document. Your decision to terminate is much less likely to provoke legal action if both you and the employee know that you have the proof to back up your claims.
- Have a clear and comprehensive employee manual and make certain the employee has read it. Having all employees sign a statement that they have read and understood the policies contained within the manual is a critical safeguard to preventing termination lawsuits.
- Make sure the punishment fits the crime. If the behavior was an isolated occurrence or was not especially egregious, consider another step before termination.
- Treat all employees equally. Whatever steps you take leading up to termination, make sure the procedures are followed uniformly within the company. If you do not enforce the rules uniformly, you are opening yourself up to legal action when you fire someone for bad behavior.
- If the firing is unusually sensitive, consult with your employment attorney every step of the way.

The Resources

As noted above, finding qualified counsel who specializes in employment law is critical and should be done at the outset. While obtaining a referral from another business colleague is often the best way to find a competent, knowledgeable attorney, other sources include *www.martindale.com*, *www.findlaw.com*, and *www.lawyers.com*.

The following are sources to help you ascertain if termination is appropriate:

www.allbusiness.com is a general business site covering many topics of interest to employers and business owners.

www.employer-employee.com covers the nitty-gritty on the relationship between employers and employees.

www.canonprofits.org provides information relating to non-profit organization that relates to for-profit corporations.

Conducting the Employee Termination Meeting

Handling an Employee Termination with Grace

One of the most difficult things you must do as a manager is tell an employee that his or her working relationship with the company must end. This step should only be a last resort. You should only terminate an employee after you have compiled and documented enough evidence and made certain you are not violating anti-discrimination laws.

The meeting to terminate the employee can be extremely challenging. The conversation is complicated with extremely high stakes, and if not handled properly can cause significant damage both to the employee and to the company. You do not want to provoke the employee either during or after the meeting. The person responsible for conducting the termination meeting must be up to the task. In some cases, the employee's manager or supervisor should handle the meeting; in other instances, it should be the owner of the company or the human resources manager. If you have a human resources department, you and your managers should work in tandem to ensure that the meeting goes smoothly. Careful coaching by human resources or the company's outside employment law specialist is critical. If those sources are not available to you, do not lose heart. By remaining cool, calm and professional, you should be able to conduct a successful termination meeting.

It goes without saying that each situation is different; however, there are certain overarching conditions that exist in almost all involuntary separations. An employee that is being terminated is likely to feel humiliated, hurt and angry. You need to make sure that there is a proper venue for the employee to express some of those feelings, but you also need to do whatever is in your power to minimize these feelings. Preserving the employee's dignity is crucial. This cannot be overemphasized. You must conduct the meeting in such a way so that the employee leaves with his or her respect intact.

The following guidelines will help you avoid common problems that can occur in an employee termination meeting:

- Have a witness present.

  This can be another manager, a human resources staff member, or your employment law specialist. The witness ensures that the termination is handled appropriately, and functions as a potential deterrent against any extreme behavior on the part of the employee.

- Keep the meeting short and be direct.

  Small talk might seem to be a good idea, but it usually just prolongs the agony. Do not try to couch what you are saying in flowery terms that might be misinterpreted. The longer you talk, the greater the chance you will say something misleading or inappropriate.

- Be professional.

  Conduct the meeting calmly and keep your composure at all times. Keep the atmosphere in the room completely business-like and treat the employee with respect and dignity. Do not disparage the employee or make light of the situation. Do not say anything in anger, no matter how much the employee pushes your buttons.

- Explain the need for termination in plain language.

  Your message should be unmistakable. Clarify why the employee did not meet expectations. Remind the employee of all the coaching and intervention that had been done on his or her behalf. Be brief; the employee may want to know some details, but in all likelihood, he or she just wants to leave. Termination should not be a complete surprise to the employee, despite his or her claims; if the employee's supervisor has documented accurately and provided timely feedback, the employee should know that termination was a possibility.

- Do not mislead or give false hope.

  Do not say anything that could be misinterpreted and thrown back to you at a later date. Make clear that your decision is final and that there is no going back. Be kind, but be careful. The employee has to understand that the door is closed.

- Do not condescend or patronize.

  This will only further aggravate the situation. At this point, the employee understands what is happening. Condescension or patronization can easily provoke a strong negative response.

- Avoid intimating that the employee did not fit into the company culture.

  Do not say anything to the employee that would lead him or her to conclude that the termination is due to race, age, birthplace, color, disability, marital/family status, national origin, religion or sex. Terminating an employee for any of these reasons is against the law; if you even hint at one of these, it is certain to bring a legal claim or lawsuit against your company.

- Have the employee fill out an exit interview form.

  If he or she balks at filling it out, explain that this is a rule and is necessary to complete the termination process. This step is important on many levels. It gives the employee an opportunity to vent in writing, which may be more comfortable than a face-to-face confrontation. You can gain valuable feedback from a terminated employee. The form also provides closure.

- Go over housekeeping issues.

  Make sure the employee gives you his or her ID card or company badge. If there is company property that needs to be returned, make sure the proper arrangements are made.

- Issue the final paycheck.

  If the termination is to take effect immediately, give the employee his or her final paycheck, but only after all outstanding company property has been recovered and the proper paperwork is in order. If there is to be an exit interview later in the day, the paycheck should be given at that time.

- Sign release forms.

  If you have given the employee severance or offered outplacement benefits, have the employee sign a release form indicating that they understand this is all that he or she will be receiving.

- Do not act high-handed.

  While it is smart business sense to have the terminated employee pack his or her things and leave as soon as possible, do not make a great show of escorting the employee to his or her desk. Have the employee escorted quietly.

- Allow the employee to say goodbye.

  Permit brief goodbyes between the employee and coworkers, but do not allow a scene or a grandstanding opportunity. This will damage morale and make a tough situation even more complicated. Do not add anything to what the employee says unless the employee says something completely outrageous.

- Wish the employee well, but only if you can do it sincerely.

  Any suggestion of disingenuousness will anger the employee and could lead to litigation at a later date.

There are also procedures to be followed after the termination meeting.

- Gather all the documentation relating to the employee, and file it for a minimum of 10 years.
- Do not state anything in a termination memo, correspondence with the state unemployment board, or reference letter that contradicts what was stated at the termination meeting or in the documents that support the firing.
- Consider offering short-term outplacement counseling. It will help the employee understand that the firing was not personal.

The Resources

By following the steps outlined above, you should be able to conduct an employee termination meeting successfully. By enabling the employee to leave your company with his dignity in place, you will have significantly decreased his or her interest in pursuing legal action and you will have preserved your company's reputation. Websites with more information include *www.toolkit.cch.com* and *www.legalmatch.com*.

Conducting the
Exit Interview

Getting Your Employees to Open Up

An exit interview is a survey or interview done with your employee when he or she leaves the company. Since most employees that resign from a company tend to leave within the first 6 months of employment, it is good business sense to meet with these employees to find out what is causing them to leave. If your questions are phrased properly and posed in a non-threatening manner in a neutral venue, you are likely to discover valuable information.

This information can be used to improve poor working conditions and decrease attrition. An exit interview has the additional benefit of giving the departing employee an opportunity for closure. Done properly, it can also enable the company to retain the employee's goodwill. You may discover that the departing employee is considering legal action and you be able to prevent this. Occasionally, an employee may even reconsider his or her decision to leave and you could find yourself in the fortunate position of not having to replace a valued employee.

While it is up to the company to offer the opportunity for an exit interview, the employee does not have to agree. Employees might feel that what they say can be used against them. They also might be less willing to participate since they know that their tenure is almost completed. Nonetheless, since an exit interview can provide you with valuable information, you need to offer it to all employees who are leaving your employment.

Some companies maintain that there is no point in conducting an exit interview with an employee that has been terminated, especially if the employee was terminated for cause. The evidence indicates otherwise. If you can remove the heated emotion from the conversation, a terminated employee can also provide insights into your working situation and help you uncover problems that you were not aware of. While you need to make sure you stick to your script, do not miss this opportunity to gain valuable information.

Whatever the reason employees leave, replacing them is expensive and time-consuming. This is why it is in your best interest to solve problems in your working environment and company culture as soon as they are uncovered. Exit interviews can help you accomplish this.

Guidelines for Conducting an Exit Interview

1. Prepare your questions in advance. Ask the same questions to each departing employee to ensure consistency in responses and to detect patterns. Make sure that your questions do not invite only yes or no answers. The questions should be open ended and invite thoughtful answers.

2. Have the interview conducted by someone in human resources. If you do not have a human resources department, have a third party or someone who is not directly involved with the employee conduct the interview. Your interviewer needs to be an excellent listener. He or she needs to pay close attention to what is being said and take care not to judge the words or the employee.

3. Get permission to take notes. Stress to the employee that you want to learn from his or her experiences and the notes will help you remember the issues discussed.

4. Be candid as to the purpose of the exit interview. Explain that you want to learn from the employee's experiences–good and bad. Make sure it is clear that you want to listen and learn. It is okay to tell the employee that you are interested in closure and maintaining a good post-employment relationship.

5. Put the employee at ease. Do not begin by asking the tough questions first. Find about the employee, his or her likes and dislikes on the job and his or her responsibilities. Most employees will not want to burn bridges and so they will cooperate. Unfortunately, unless you really enable them to open up, you will find yourself with generic non-answers that do not help you at all. The most successful exit interview is where the employee gives you information that you can use and both parties feel good about the exchange.

6. Ask open-ended questions. If the employee is only giving you yes or no answers or can answer your questions in a few words, re-do your questions for the next time.

Points to Raise in an Exit Interview

1. Specific questions about the skills and experience needed to perform the employee's former duties need to be asked. Besides an opportunity to gain information to help the next employee, these types of questions help put the employee at ease.

2. Ask the reasons an employee is leaving. Employees tend to resign from a company for four primary reasons:
   a. A sought-after new career opportunity;
   b. an unsolicited job offer;
   c. more money or better benefits; or
   d. unresolved problems on the job that have become untenable.

3. Questions regarding management policies and philosophy and style also need to be asked. This should include questions on adequacy of training, availability of mentors and general employment and promotion opportunities.

4. Ask about general areas of improvement in the company. Although the answers to these questions may be tough to hear, it is critical to address these issues if you want to improve your working environment. Areas of improvement can include general working conditions, amount of work to do, company culture and attitude, flex-time and other benefits.

Sample questions to ask in an exit interview

- What did you like most about your job?
- What did you like least about your job?
- What parts of your job worked?
- What parts were not successful?
- Were your initial job expectations in line with the actual job duties?
- Did your manager support or undermine you?
- What was the quality of the supervision you received?
- How could your immediate supervisor improve his performance?
- Did you receive sufficient feedback about your performance?
- Were you happy with the company's merit review, raise and promotion processes?
- Did you receive adequate training to be successful in your job?
- What do you think it takes to be successful at your job?
- What do you think it takes to be successful at this company?
- Was the work evenly distributed?
- Were there internal or external issues that made your job harder?
- Do you feel that the company benefit package was inadequate, adequate or superior?
- What is your primary reason for leaving?
- Was there a particular event that caused you to leave?
- Did this company help you to fulfill your career goals?
- Do you have suggestions as to qualities we should be looking for in your replacement?
- What suggestions do you have to help us improve our workplace?
- Did you feel our pay scale was below, at or above market?

- How do you generally feel about this company?
- What did you like the best about this company?
- What did you like the least about this company?
- Would you ever work for this company again?
- Would you ever recommend working for this company to your family and friends?
- What does your new company offer that this company does not?
- Can this company do anything to encourage you to stay?
- Before deciding to leave, did you check out other positions within the company?
- Did anyone in this company discriminate against you, harass you or cause hostile working conditions?
- Do you have any other comments?

There are some questions in the above list that are not appropriate or relevant if the employee has been fired, but the majority can be asked under any circumstances. It is important to realize that the answers you receive may not necessarily be completely truthful, but regardless these questions need to be asked.

Some companies give the employee the option of an exit interview conducted via telephone after the employee has left. While this type of interview can give the employee more privacy enabling him or her to speak more freely, typically the interest level is not the same. In all likelihood, the employee will be more than ready to move on and simply less willing to participant in an exercise giving him or her little or no tangible benefit.

Regardless of the format of the exit interview, the results should be documented and tabulated. Keeping track of the responses and the trends that they demonstrate are the most valuable part of the exit interview process. The information that departing employees can provide, especially if they show trends and patterns that can be fixed will be well worth the time you spend creating and asking your questions.

The Resources

For general information regarding exit interviews, see:

http://workforce.com

www.managementhelp.org

Employee Misstating Qualifications

How Serious Is the Problem?

Every applicant who submits a resume wants to attract your attention by presenting their best skills and experience. There is, in all resumes, a degree of persuasive marketing, the ability to explain a candidate's skills in light of the job being sought, and an active sales effort to show why he or she is the best candidate.

Misstating information can be unintentional; for example, listing an incorrect date or job title in a resume. It can also be quite intentional, meaning that the applicant will use any means possible to improve his or her chances of gaining employment. Even among those who misrepresent the facts, there can be extremes: from the proverbial white lie (e.g., enhanced salary) to gross misrepresentation (e.g., claming an advanced degree which was never earned).

Lying on resumes is apparently on the rise. According to a Knight-Ridder-Tribune Business News article, an online survey conducted by the Society for Human Resource Management determined that more than 60 percent of human resource professionals found inaccuracies on resumes. In another online survey, conducted by Korn/Ferry, nearly half the respondents said they believed resume fraud among executives is increasing.

Is misrepresenting one's qualifications marketing or downright deception? Is there a difference? Do you, as an owner or manager, care about this kind of activity? Do you dismiss it, assuming that everyone exaggerates in some way? Where do you draw the line between creative marketing and fraud? Some individuals unnecessarily exaggerate their qualifications. For instance, a high-profile football coach was recently offered a job in a prestigious college football program; he ultimately resigned after college administrators learned that he claimed an advanced degree that he never earned. He was not hired for this degree, but rather for his 20 years of successful teams and coaching. Why the need to embellish when the job was his? There seemingly is a compulsion on the part of even highly successful individuals to cover some flaw, real or imagined.

More pragmatically, most lying on resumes reflects the competitive job market, especially for prime positions or jobs with successful, reputable companies. Employers are partly responsible for this growing trend, because they look for better credentials and more experience than is needed for the job. Because many employers never go beyond the resume in rejecting employees, prospects have no opportunity to sell themselves in any other way. If an applicant does not make a good first impression, he or she will never even get to the interview stage.

What are some of the typical misrepresentations? Consider some of the responses to that question from employment experts:

- Length of industry experience.
- Misrepresenting accomplishments.
- Exaggerating the number of people in their department or those they supervised.
- Reasons for leaving a previous job (which should not be in a resume in the first place).
- Exaggerating salary, knowing that it is difficult to prove otherwise.
- Changing employment dates to cover a period of unemployment.

Applicants often justify these kinds of misrepresentations because they assume that everyone else is overstating accomplishments. Prospective employees worry that not having a certain degree or the exact experience that companies seek means that they will not be offered an interview, much less a job. Experts and professionals who advise job applicants urge people not to lie on resumes and not to exaggerate the facts. It is a simple matter for an employee to verify whether an applicant earned his or her stated degree.

What You Should Do if You Discover an Employee Has Lied?

As a general rule, you should be more concerned about resume exaggerations in relation to employee seniority. The senior person you wish to add to your staff must be above reproach. If he or she lied on a resume, it could be that he or she will falsify company documents.

Ask yourself what lying or exaggeration says about an individual. Was this a small matter that can be set aside because of the employee's 2 years of quality work, indicating that the lie was likely a one-time event in a moment of weakness? If a person lies on a resume, can he or she be trusted? Does this individual reflect your organization's values? What happens if word gets out to other employees (and it often does) that a new hire has misrepresented either experience or background? What effect will this have on morale?

The problem is further compounded if you have hired a key employee and you discover that the individual lied or exaggerated his or her experience on a resume. Further assume that this individual is doing a good job. If you fire this person immediately, you will have lost an effective employee, will have a hole in your management team, and will incur the expense, time and effort to search for a replacement.

One approach is to assume that an otherwise competent employee can be salvaged. The individual should be confronted with your findings, some record of the problem should be placed in the employee's file, and some form of remediation should take place to ensure the similar lapses will not occur. It might be a good idea to put the employee on probation for a period of time, with regular reviews of both his or her ethical conduct and work performance.

A second approach is simply to state that your organization has a zero-tolerance approach to any form of misrepresentation, including exaggeration of one's credentials. This is one of the reasons for an employment application, as these forms typically include a statement that lying on an application is grounds for dismissal. After the facts are verified and the employee is confronted with the facts, he or she is terminated immediately without severance. Further, the reasons for the dismissal should be communicated to other employees after the fact, either through a memo or a company-wide meeting.

Whatever your company policy regarding lying and misrepresentation, your offers for employment should always be contingent upon successful completion of a thorough background check.

Your Best Strategy is Prevention

The best approach is to avoid those situations in which employees have misrepresented themselves. Firms that specialize in background verification can assist you to investigate a prospective employee's credentials, including dates of previous employment, academic degrees, professional honors, published articles, and so forth.

As a manager, you must ensure that every person you hire is thoroughly checked, either by in-house personnel, the search firm that referred the employee to you, or an outside agency. Internet searches can also provide a great deal of information on prospective employees. It is important that you question previous colleagues, references and former employers. If you suspect misrepresentation, interview the employee again and ask for further information about that area of concern. Focus on this issue when you conduct reference and background checks.

Misrepresentation of credentials is a growing problem, so much so that many states either have or are initiating laws against individuals who exaggerate on resumes and employment applications.

The Resources

Make it standard practice to get a prospective employee's permission to check his or her personal and professional backgrounds. A complete set of authorization forms can be purchased from online legal suppliers like Nolo by visiting *www.nolo.com.*

The Complete Reference Checking Handbook: Smart, Fast, Legal Ways to Check out Job Applicants (Amacom, 1998) is an excellent source on how to conduct a thorough reference check. You can obtain this book at *www.amazon.com* or other online retailers.

Worker Adjustment & Retraining Notification

Giving Advance Notice of a Closing or Mass Layoff

The Worker Adjustment and Retraining Notification Act of 1988 (WARN) requires most employers with 100 or more employees to provide 60 calendar days of notification to affected employees in advance of plant closings or mass layoffs.

Managers, supervisors, and both hourly and salaried employees are entitled to the 60-day advance notice under the WARN Act. The Act also requires that notice be given to:

- Affected employees or their representatives;
- the local chief elected government official; and
- the state dislocated worker unit.

Regular federal, state and local government entities that provide public services are not subject to the WARN Act.

The WARN Act is intended to give workers and their family time to adjust to the upcoming loss of employment. The 60-day period gives affected employees time to seek other jobs or upgrade their skills through training programs.

Specific provisions of the WARN Act include the following:

1. Plant Closings

   WARN defines a plant closing as a temporary or permanent shutdown of an entire single site or one or more facilities or operating units within a single employment site. The shutdown must result in an employment loss during any 30-day period for 50 or more full-time employees in order to qualify as a plant closing.

2. Mass Layoffs

   WARN defines a mass layoff as a reduction in force (not a plant closing) during any 30-day period that results in the employment loss at a single employment site for either 50 or more full-time employees (if they compose 33 percent of the workforce at the employment site), or 500 or more full-time employees.

3. Employment Loss

WARN defines employment loss as the involuntary termination of employment (other than for cause), layoff for more than 6 months, or at least a 50 percent reduction in hours for each month of a 6-month period. Part-time employees are excluded by definition and are not counted in the required numbers of 50 or 500. Part-time employees are those who work fewer than 20 hours per week or who have been employed for fewer than 6 months in the 12 months preceding the date on which the notice is required.

Employers are also required to give notice if the number of employment losses that occur during a 30-day period fails to meet the threshold requirement of a plant closing or mass layoff, but the number of employment losses for two or more groups of workers (each of which is less than the minimum number needed to trigger notice), reaches the threshold level during any 90-day period of either a plant closing or a mass layoff. Losses of jobs within a 90-day period will count together toward WARN thresholds, unless the employer can prove that losses during the 90-day period are the result of separate causes.

Sale of a Business

The following requirements apply in a situation involving the full or partial sale of a business:

1. In all sale situations, there is always an employer responsible for giving notice.

2. If the sale results in a plant closing or mass layoff, employees must be given 60 days notice.

3. The seller is required to give the 60-day notice up to and including the date and time of the sale.

4. The buyer is required to give the 60-day notice if the plant closing or mass layoffs occur after date/time of the sale.

5. No notice is required if the sale does not result in a closing or layoff.

6. Employees of the seller become employees of the buyer for purposes of WARN immediately following the sale. This preserves the notification rights of employees of businesses that have been sold.

Exceptions

An employer does not need to give notice if:

1. A plant closing is the closing of a temporary facility, or if the closing is the result of the completion of a particular project or undertaking.

2. No notice needs to be given to strikers or to workers who are part of the bargaining unit that is involved in the labor negotiations that led to a lockout when the strike is equivalent to a plant closing or mass layoff. Nonstriking workers are entitled to a notice.

3. An employer does not need to give notice when permanently replacing a person who is an economic striker as defined by the National Labor Relations Act.

Notice must be timed to reach the required parties at least 60 days before a closing or mass layoff with three exceptions:

1. A faltering company: Covers situations where a company has sought new capital or business in order to stay open, and where notice would jeopardize the opportunity to obtain new capital.

2. Unforeseeable business circumstances: Applicable to closings or layoffs caused by circumstances that were not reasonably foreseeable at the time the notice would have been otherwise required.

3. Natural disaster: Applicable to closings or layoffs caused by natural disasters such as floods, earthquakes, hurricanes or tornadoes.

If an employer gives less than 60 days notice, one of the above exceptions must apply, and the burden of proof lies with the employer. Employers using an exception must give as much notice as is possible and practical to fit the extenuating circumstance.

Form and Content

Employers should be aware that all notices to the required parties must be in writing. Any method of delivery is acceptable, provided that the notice arrives at least 60 days before closing or layoff. The content of the notices is listed in section 639.7 of the WARN final regulations. To learn more see The Resouces at the end of this chapter.

The notice may include additional information useful to the employees such as information on available dislocated worker assistance, and, if the planned action is expected to be temporary, the estimated duration, if known.

Penalties

Employers who violate the WARN provisions by ordering a plant closing or mass layoff without proper notice are liable to each aggrieved employee for an amount including back pay and benefits for the period of the violation, up to 60 days. An employer who fails to provide notice to a unit of the local government may be subject to a civil penalty of up to $500 for each violation day.

The Resources

The U.S. Department of Labor provides a useful fact sheet on the WARN Act at *www.doleta.gov/programs/factsht/warn.htm.*

The Office of Compliance lists the complete WARN Act final regulations at *www.compliance.gov/employeerights/reg_masslayoff.html.*
You may also call the U.S. Department of Labor at 1.202.219.5577.

Separation Letters

The Overview

Few people look forward to being fired. There are basically three reasons for termination: poor performance, downsizing, and office closings, in which employment separation agreements generally accompany a termination notice.

A separation letter may also be called a termination agreement, severance agreement, separation agreement, or general release. The separation letter should be unique to the individual, because each situation is unique. A one-size-fits-all or checklist form of separation letter is callous and if the termination is due to an office closing or layoff situation, the letter does not acknowledge the value the employee brought to the employment relationship.

The wording of a separation letter will be different for each situation. It is important that your termination letter be carefully written because:

- It eases the pain for an employee who will have to make an often difficult transition to new employment;
- the written word is easily preserved and can come back to haunt you;
- it will reflect well on your company as signs of courtesy and professionalism;
- it can help reduce hostility if it does not openly reproach the employee;
- it gives the employee the benefit of the doubt for facts not in evidence; and
- circumstances may change and you may wish to rehire the same employee.

Separation letters should be written and signed by the highest-ranking member of your company to dispel any hope the employee may have of appealing the decision to the next level of management. Avoid sending letters signed by a junior officer or the head of your human resources department.

Depending on the specifics of your situation, there are several important components that should be included in a separation letter or in an accompanying packet:

- the company name and address
- effective date of termination
- severance benefits, including the type and when they will be given
- health, disability or life insurance coverage or conversion, including COBRA benefits
- final pay, including any bonuses, accrued benefits for sick leave
- outplacement help (use of the office, secretarial support, etc.)
- treatment of vested stock options
- information about retirement plans, health savings accounts, childcare or transportation savings accounts
- releases for the employee to sign, including noncompete, confidentiality and/or nondisclosure agreements
- expense reimbursement for any outstanding expenses owed the employee
- reference agreement

Composing a letter can be one of the most difficult writing exercises you will have to do. Regardless of the reason for the letter, the tone should be one of sensitivity, tact, concern and appreciation for the employee's work or empathy for their termination. Begin by summarizing the employee's history with the organization. Then be truthful, straightforward, objective and clear in stating any reasons for dismissal.

- As much as you may like to, do not apologize for the company's decision or include personal apologies. Avoid false or ambiguous statements, even if meant to protect the employee's ego, as they may be used against you if your decision is later challenged. If you do not include all the reasons for termination in a letter to the employee, do include a full explanation in your files including any backup documentation you have.
- Let the employee know your company will release only job titles, salary and date of employment to prospective employers if it is your company's policy to withhold other details about performance and reasons for termination.
- Avoid a hostile tone; instead show concern for the employee's future well-being.

A sample termination letter for poor performance may look like this:

Confidential

June 20XX

Dear Ms. Smith:

In conjunction with our conversations about your behavior, you have received three disciplinary notices within the past 6 months. Unfortunately, we have not see a change in your performance or behavior. In the last year you have been late 41 times, absent without excuse on 10 occasions, and late on all but one project deadlines.

It is important to the company's success and that of our clients that employees are punctual and conscientious about attendance and deadlines. Our clients will look elsewhere if we cannot offer them reliable service. You have demonstrated an unacceptable pattern of behavior. Thus, we can no longer continue your employment at ABC Company, Inc.

This decision is irrevocable. You will be paid 2 weeks salary. Our policy is to give only title of position and dates of employment to companies seeking references. You can be assured the details of this situation will remain strictly a company matter.

Sincerely,

Company President

A sample layoff letter may look like this:

Confidential

June 20XX

Dear Sandy:

It is with sincere regret that I must inform you that your employment at ABC Company, Inc. will be terminated as of Friday, January 31.

As you know, the financial task force delivered their report to the general manager in late October. One of the recommendations proposed by the task force was the elimination of all temporary and contract positions. Since you occupy a temporary position, your position is automatically subject to the task force recommendations.

I would like to make it absolutely clear in no way does your termination reflect that any displeasure with your work performance over the past 18 months. In fact, you have been highly regarded as one of our most productive contract staffers. Unfortunately, the fact you and the other nonpermanent staff that are being let go is simply a reflection of the general economic downturn in the manufacturing industry over the past decade.

In an effort to lessen the impact of this termination, the company has worked out a severance arrangement that will give you 1 week's pay for each month you worked beyond 12 months. In your case you will receive 6 weeks of severance pay. In addition, your medical and dental coverage will remain in effect until the end of the severance period. Within the next week you will receive a letter from the human resources department outlining the details of your severance package.

Given your qualifications and proven abilities, Sandy, I am confident that you will be able to find another position in the relatively near future. The services of the outsourcing company Schuler and Hoffman are at your disposal should you need resume, cover letter or research assistance. I will be pleased to write a recommendation letter for you to aid in your job search.

Sincerely,

Company President

A sample office-closing letter may look like this:

Confidential

June

Dear Fred:

It is with sincere regret that I must inform you that ABC Company, Inc. will be merging with DEF Company, Inc. and moving the offices to Florida on January 31. As a result, ABC Company will close its Atlanta offices effective January 31, and all employment positions will be eliminated at the Atlanta location as of that date.

I would like to thank you for your dedication and support of ABC Company. Unfortunately, this merger has created duplication of staff functions. In an effort to eliminate job redundancy, the elimination of these staff positions is simply a product of the merger.

In an effort to lessen the impact of this termination, the company has worked out a severance arrangement that will give you 1 week's pay for each month you worked beyond 12 months. In your case you will receive 6 weeks of severance pay. In addition, your medical and dental coverage will remain in effect until the end of the severance period. Within the next week you will receive a letter from the human resources department outlining the details of your severance package.

Given your qualifications and proven abilities, I am confident that you will be able to find another position in the relatively near future. The services of an outsourcing company are at your disposal should you need resume, cover letter or research assistance. I will be pleased to write a recommendation letter for you to aid in your job search.

Sincerely,

Company President

Employee terminations for any reason are difficult for every employee. They affect morale company-wide, both for those terminated and for those who remain employed. Advanced preparation of materials will make it easier for everyone.

The Resources

Create your own termination or separation letter online at Law Depot: *www.lawdepot.com/contracts/termination/?ad=employ_related*.

Visit the Lawyers.com Website at *www.lawyers.com/lawyers/A~1001854~LDS/JOB+TERMINATION.html*, for legal FAQs regarding employee terminations.

What Not To Say or Do When Terminating an Employee

Firing an Employee Without Provoking a Lawsuit or Worse

After carefully reading the applicable laws, conferring with your employment attorney, and checking that your documentation is complete, you decide that there is no recourse but to terminate the employee.

Terminating is never easy. Most managers agree that firing an employee is one of the hardest tasks they face. There is failure on both sides: failure of the employee to perform and failure of the employer or manager to coach adequately. No matter how poor the employee's performance was, most employers feel a certain amount of guilt when they have to let someone go, even if it is for cause. Some managers choose to fire an employee the first thing in the morning just to relieve their own stress. Breaking up personal and business relationships is difficult. Further complicating matters, the employee is dependent upon the employer for income. So you wonder in a panic, knowing how upset the employee is going to be, how to ensure that the employee will not retaliate with a lawsuit, or even worse, by responding violently?

You can run into trouble despite the fact that you have taken all necessary steps and have not violated any laws. No matter how kindly you have treated your employee, he or she may sue you or react with violence he or she realizes that you will not reconsider. What you can do is try to do your best and manage those factors that are within your control. You also must choose each word with the utmost care to make certain that your words do not come back to haunt you. You need to try to make a painful situation as painless as possible for you and for the employee.

It is often stated that the best defense is a good offense. In this case, it means that you have to have a plan. Take adequate time to prepare, have all your facts and documentation ready to access, and take things slowly. It does not matter if you feel like you cannot wait another moment to get rid of this poor performer;

you cannot let your emotions dictate your behavior because there is too much at stake. Plan to keep it brief and to the point and to say as little as possible.

Once the decision has been made, there are some steps you can take to make the process go as smoothly as possible:

- Find the right time. Schedule the appointment in your office, towards the end of the day, and preferably on a Friday. It is best to terminate an employee when there are fewer people around. Once you decide on an appointment time, you need to keep it.

- Tell only those employees that absolutely need to know beforehand, such as those in human resources, payroll, and possibly information technology.

- Have the employee's final paycheck in hand. This not only helps drive home the finality of the decision, but also ensures that the employee will not worry whether he or she will receive a final paycheck.

The most important part of the process is the actual meeting itself. Do not assign this difficult task to one of the employee's co-workers; a manager or owner must conduct the meeting. A badly handled termination meeting is almost certain to bring legal headaches and trouble later.

Planning what you have to say is helpful. It helps you avoid saying things that you should not, and it can often relieve some of the anxiety and stress that go along with the burden of having to terminate an employee. Trying to anticipate the reaction of the employee is also beneficial. If you believe that the employee is likely to break down, he or she may appreciate having tissues at hand. If you suspect that the employee may react violently, security should be alerted beforehand and remain nearby. It is critical that you remain in control of the meeting, and the better prepared you are, the more likely that you will remain in control. It is also helpful to have a witness present, preferably another manager or a human resources representative.

Determining what not to say is as important as considering what should be said. The following are guidelines to follow and examples of what you should not say to the employee:

- Do not make a lot of small talk. The employee will not appreciate discussing the weather when the true purpose of the meeting is revealed.

- Do not tell the employee that you are cutting staff unless you truly are. If the employee discovers later that what you said was untrue, he or she will begin looking for another reason for the termination. If the employee suspects discrimination, he or she may file suit.

- Do not say that the employee did not fit in or that you are changing your company image. Both of these reasons reflect the composition of the company, which sounds like discrimination.

- Do not mention the employee's physical condition in any way. Again, this will be opening the door to a discrimination lawsuit.

- Do not tell someone that he or she is not a team player. This invites a debate and you could be drawn into something that you will regret later.

- Do not mock or belittle the employee and do not make jokes. These actions will anger the employee and can provoke an extreme reaction.

- Do not respond angrily to anything that is said. The employee is trying to gall you into saying something that he or she can use in a claim against you. As difficult as it may be, you need to remain calm, cool and objective.

- Explain the reasons for the termination in simple terms. Do not say, you are fired, or any other slang expression, but use a more neutral method to tell the employee that he or she is released from employment.

- Do not say anything that can be misconstrued. Make sure that the employee understands that this is not a negotiation and the door is closed. Saying things such as: If only you had…or I am sorry things did not work out can lead the employee to believe that the situation can be reversed. You may be trying to soften the blow, but once someone is told that they being terminated, he or she will probably have a hard time concentrating and may only hear part of what you are trying to articulate.

- Do not patronize the employee by telling them you understand or how difficult this is for you; this is offensive and belittling and is likely to provoke anger.

Treating a terminated employee with respect and consideration will go a long way in preventing legal claims and lawsuits. Taking the time to plan what you have to say and to envisioning how someone will actually hear your words will help you end an employer-employee relationship with minimal damage to your former employee's ego and to your company.

The Resources

General business Websites such as *www.allbusiness.com*, *www.businesstown.com*, and *http://smallbusiness.yahoo.com* provide more information about this delicate subject.

Downsizing

The Reality

Businesses are infinitely creative when it comes to manufacturing words that try to soften the impact of negative news. Downsizing is one of the classics in organizational jargon–much easier and more pleasant than layoffs, unemployment or termination. No matter how one tries to sugarcoat it, the fact is that downsizing means some employees are going–perhaps even an entire plant or regional office. Alternative related concepts are rightsizing and reengineering, also both basically terms that suggest some change in not only the size of the company but the organizational chart and ultimately the culture of the enterprise.

Whatever term you prefer to use, layoffs (assuming more than just a few employees) are so common place that we accept them almost without a blink. Of course, the employees who are downsized because of a plant closing or for competitive reasons have the same reaction as anyone: a gut wrenching sense that their families and their economic futures are in jeopardy.

No rational manager downsizes without a good business reason. Common reasons are:

- The organization has fallen behind the competition.
- The cost of doing business is too high.
- Total company productivity is lower than it should be.
- Too many people were hired during periods of growth.
- Technological changes have made jobs obsolete.
- The organization has lost a major client or contract.
- The company strategy has changed, and new businesses are being built to replace old ones.
- Government regulations or environmental issues have forced a plant to close.
- Management has been slow to respond to the changing business environment.

- Collective bargaining agreements have changed, allowing for changes in the employee mix.
- Planned merger with another company.
- An effort to impress shareholders and the financial community by reducing overhead.
- A company is in bankruptcy.

In a perfect world, large-scale downsizing would never happen, as organizations would constantly adapt to the changing economic and business environment. Of course, this is not a perfect world, and there are times when an enterprise cannot anticipate changes which will affect employment.

Good Business Reasons

It is incorrect that downsizing always results in cost savings for an organization; in fact, there is substantial evidence that it does not. It is preferable for an organization to periodically adjust its employee numbers, not only through terminations, but also by hiring conservatively.

Management may use downsizing to signal that they are in charge and are prepared to make sacrifices to ensure the future health of the enterprise. This activity may have nothing to do with the organization's employment needs. Further, downsizing can be a means of reducing older workers, with the aim to replace them in the future with younger and less expensive workers. (Here, certainly, you must have strong proof that your actions do not discriminate against older workers.)

In certain situations, downsizing has nothing to do with economics, but rather a need (real or perceived) to improve the bottom line in the short term. You may decide to lay off employees to ensure that investors, banks, and other key groups are comfortable with management, its policies and strategies. Even the most profitable companies in the best economic times shed employees–many of whom they probably need.

Downsizing Changes an Organization

Whether your employees number in the hundreds or thousands, downsizing–even reducing the workforce by 5 percent or 10 percent–will change your company's culture and environment. Nothing will be the same after multiple layoffs.

What are some of the consequences of downsizing on the enterprise?

- Morale suffers: employees who are retained naturally wonder if more layoffs are coming.

- Productivity will suffer, as commitment to and enthusiasm for the company wanes.
- Management will spend an enormous amount of time and effort working with the remaining employees, as work is reassigned and departments are realigned.
- Unless the downsizing is handled well, labor lawsuits are inevitable.
- Key employees who were retained may decide to leave for other employment.
- Workloads may increase to the point where current employees refuse to work overtime or on weekends.
- Management is perceived as not caring, insensitive or incompetent.
- Trust and loyalty are lost.

There are circumstances that cannot be helped. As a rule, however, you should think seriously before announcing a large layoff, because the ramifications of such an event often exceed expectations.

How to Handle Downsizing

If you must initiate a drastic staff reduction for valid reasons, be honest and sensitive to your employees' concerns. Face them directly, personally, and with an established plan to assist them during the transition. Severance benefits, re-employment assistance, outplacement counseling, and letters of reference can go a long way to soothe some of the anger and hurt your employees will likely feel.

It is essential that news of a significant downsizing be kept confidential until a final decision has been made and a plan is in place. You want to avoid information leaks which will become grist for the rumor mill. Nothing destroys an organization quicker than rumors about impending layoffs.

Key managers involved in downsizing decisions must ensure that discussions are kept confidential; if necessary, conduct the initial discussion off-site. The management team should be as small as possible, ideally only the top two or three people in the organization. The day before the announcement, other managers may be invited to discuss plans for individual workers within the department—that is, who will be retained and who will be laid off.

Everything must be in order the day of the announcement. If voluntary retirement is part of the plan, individual offers must be ready. You may find that, if enough employees take the buyout option, you may not need to further reduce your staff.

At this time, you should make arrangements for employees to leave the premises, typically at the end of the day. Have employees schedule appointments for paperwork, severance, and outplacement services on an individual basis. Terminated employees should not be allowed to remain on the premises for too long a time; delays may result in retaliation and even poorer morale for those who were retained.

Management's real concerns are for the employees who remain, how the departments will function, new reporting responsibilities, and bolstering morale. Schedule company-wide or departmental meetings to explain why layoffs were necessary, and whether more are planned. Hopefully, you will do it right the first time; nothing would be worse than gradual, periodic layoffs.

Insist that department heads meet with their teams to answer questions and allow employees to vent their frustration and anger. After the initial period of shock and anger, managers must meet with remaining employees individually or in small groups to clarify jobs and responsibilities and to rebuild morale. Share information about sales, profits and company performance so that people understand the circumstances. Carefully monitor the reactions and behaviors of your retained employees, and be ready to intervene to keep them as employees.

The Resources

Because managing the company and its employees after downsizing is your most important task, consider *The New Corporate Cultures: Revitalizing the Workplace after Downsizing, Mergers and Reengineering* (Perseus Books Group, 2000). This book discusses in detail how to balance company needs with employee expectations and concerns. This and similar books can be found by visiting *www.amazon.com* or other online vendors.

Firing Union Employees

Working with Union Organizations

The involuntary termination of a union employee is a more complicated situation than firing a nonunion employee. A union has a collective bargaining agreement with an employer, and along with that agreement comes a number of contractual policies and procedures. It is vital that all levels of management fully understand those policies and procedures that the company agreed to in the union contract. A member of management who fails to follow an agreed-upon policy of the contract can seriously jeopardize management efforts to justifiably fire a union employee. Most union contracts allow management the right to fire at-will during the typical 60- to 90-day probationary period. But once a union employee passes that probationary period, the collective bargaining agreement terms and conditions take effect and at-will status no longer applies. It is important to fully document your decision, which must be based on just cause. Documenting just cause protects the employer in case the fired employee decides to sue for wrongful discharge or breach of contract.

When attempting to fire a union employee, it is best to follow the same steps of progressive discipline that would be afforded a nonunion employee. Title VII of the Civil Rights Act of 1964 protects union and nonunion employees from discrimination in the firing process. This applies regardless of any policies laid out in a bargaining agreement or labor contract. Firings are illegal when based on age, sex, national origin, union membership, or any other legally protected class.

Employers should review their collective bargaining agreements for language that covers progressive discipline for union employees. An example of those steps that may be in a collective bargaining agreement are as follows:

Step 1: Oral warning, documented and signed by all parties.
Step 2: First written warning, documented and signed by all parties.
Step 3: Second written warning, documented and signed by all parties.

Step 4: Final written warning, documented and signed by all parties.

Step 5: Firing for the reasons documented.

Progressive discipline is usually accompanied by unpaid time off that increases as the steps progress. Employees disciplined for attendance problems are usually not rewarded with disciplinary time off.

Acts of gross misconduct such as theft, willful property damage or fighting are just causes for firing; progressive discipline is not required in these circumstances. A thorough investigation must take place and should be completed within 24 to 48 hours after the problem arises. The employee should be informed as to the results 24 to 48 hours thereafter. In a union environment, the contractual agreement usually calls for intervention by a union representative before a firing occurs. The representative will ensure that the terms of the collective bargaining agreement will be followed, especially those terms specific to the grievance procedure.

Grievance Procedure and The Weingarten Act

A grievance is a disagreement between a union employee and management. Typically, the sides disagree on alleged violations of contract provisions, work rules, or violations of the law, or when an employee perceives that he or she is receiving unfair disciplinary treatment.

The steps in the grievance process are:

1. The union employee files a grievance with the immediate supervisor.

2. The employee, immediate supervisor, and union steward attempt to resolve the grievance.

3. The grievance escalates to the next levels of the union and the company.

4. A neutral outside arbitrator may be called in to settle the issue. Approximately 98 percent of all collective bargaining agreements call for binding arbitration.

The Weingarten Rule stipulates that if a union employee believes that meeting with a supervisor or being questioned during an investigation may result in disciplinary action against them, they have the right to a representative. Union employees have the right to request a union delegate, and that delegate should be required to sign warning notices issued to employees whom they represent. In 2004 the National Labor Relations Board ruled that the Weingarten Rule applies only to union employees.

Management should have a witness at the meeting in which the union employee will be fired. The proceedings should be fully documented. It is also advisable to have the employee sign the termination document; all other parties present at the meeting should also sign.

The importance of documentation cannot be emphasized in terms of firing an employee, whether union or nonunion. If an employee sues for wrongful discharge and claims discrimination or unfair treatment, appropriate documentation of the facts will save you time and money. After all, the written word offers far more persuasive proof than a verbal exchange.

The Resources

For more information about the Weingarten case (NLRB vs. Weingarten, 420 U.S. 251 [1975]), visit *www.shrm.org*.

Severance

Where to Start

There is a general expectation that some form of severance package is appropriate for terminated employees, except those who were fired for cause. The topic of severance involves conflicting laws, regulations, theories and practices. There are literally dozens of variables that determine who should receive severance, and if so, what it should be.

As a rule, you are under no obligation to offer any kind of severance package to departing employees. However, in some states there may be regulations that affect the closing of a plant or laying off a large number of employees at one time. In these cases, some form of severance may be required, although the amount to be paid is not specified–nor should it be.

You may also be required to provide severance by prior agreement with an employee on a preexisting employment agreement or contract. Believe it or not, an oral promise may be binding if witnessed by others; be aware of any policies in the employment contract or anything that has been promised an employee.

An employee may make a claim–legal and moral–for severance if you have a stated policy in your employee handbook or personnel policies. Further, if your company has a history of offering severance to all fired employees, by any decent standard you should be prepared to offer a package to everyone who is laid off.

It is important to remember that severance is not just necessarily pay–although that is usually the most important element for the fired employee. Severance may also include continuation of insurance benefits, providing offices for employment searches, outplacement services, counseling, or letters of recommendation. In some situations, the right to retain one's health insurance is the most important benefit (e.g., where an employee or dependent is in poor health). The Consolidated Omnibus Budget Reconciliation Act (COBRA) requires certain employers to offer healthcare coverage at the employee's expense. Some states have their own rules concerning health care coverage, so check with the local state department of labor to ensure that you are in compliance.

A Severance Plan May Be Good Business

Severance may not be good business if the enterprise is in precarious financial condition. You cannot promise to pay something that you do not have. If sales, cash flow, and general business conditions are forcing layoffs, as is often the case, you may simply not be able to offer even a modest severance package.

However, assuming your organization is not on the brink of bankruptcy, a severance plan is good policy and generally good business. If nothing else, it helps relieve guilt on the part of the employer and stress on the part of the employee. Severance is particularly appropriate for long-term employees, as they clearly have contributed to the organization during their tenure. While you may be motivated to offer severance as a means to manage the situation, do not go overboard. Some firings are so emotional or so difficult (if concerning a relative, early member of the team, a partner) that to alleviate guilt, you may go well beyond what is prudent and reasonable.

Severance can be good business as a means to managing employee morale, and to ensure that the company does not gain a reputation for not caring about their employees' welfare. Word gets around fast, especially within your industry or in the local area. Excellent candidates for other positions may decline to accept a position because they have knowledge (personal or otherwise) of your company's past treatment of its employees.

Severance can be a means of preventing lawsuits, especially if the terminated employee is in a protected class—a minority, a woman, or an older worker, for example. An employee who feels that he or she was treated reasonably, despite the loss of a job, is less likely to seek the services of a labor lawyer. The cost of even the most frivolous lawsuit can be prohibitive, and the outcome is never predictable.

The Need for a Written Policy

If you decide that a severance plan is appropriate, you should put it in writing. It should be fair and consistent. One of the best ways to construct a policy is to tie severance benefits to years of service; that is, long-term employees would receive more than someone who was hired, say, less than a year ago. You can also structure the plan to compensate exempt employees (executives, managers, and professionals) differently from non-exempt employees (clerical and production workers).

You have the legal right to contest a former employee's request for unemployment benefits, unless the person was fired for cause. Your company may have a policy not to challenge an employment application; this is one policy that should not be written down, as it is a decision that should be made on a case-by-case basis. Why cause further hard feelings by making it difficult or impossible for the employee to collect unemployment?

A severance plan may include intangible benefits of minimal cost that will help transition your employees and improve morale. Outplacement services may not be in the budget, especially if you are a small company, but you can provide a general reference letter, the language of which should be mutually agreeable. Exercise some caution here, but if it is crafted well you should have no problems.

Asking an employee what he or she might need to help in the transition is a welcome gesture. You may find that small, simple accommodations go a long way. Forgiving advances or moving expenses, or releasing an employee from a non-compete agreement, are examples of customizing a severance package to enhance goodwill. Even allowing a former employee to keep a laptop, personal organizer, or cell phone (assuming he or she pays the bill) is not unreasonable. If this equipment is a few years old, it has little real value, and such items can be supplied to new employees at very little expense. Of course, you want to remove all company information and contacts from any equipment you give away.

Any severance pay or plan should be accompanied by a letter or agreement, signed by both parties, that outlines the exact nature of the severance. The letter should include a release that the employee will not sue your company. This release is important, as it offers some protection from lawsuits, frivolous or otherwise. In general, a release should be required whenever severance is offered, even if you are convinced that the terminated employee is not inclined to sue. You can never tell.

You cannot ask the employee to surrender a right without compensation, so the release should offer something extra if the former employee is willing to sign. You must be clear as to what rights the employee is waiving. Also, you cannot coerce the employee to sign the release. You should not provide severance until the release is signed, sealed and delivered. You need to give the employee time to consider the matter, perhaps a week or two. Older workers should receive special consideration; in such cases, it may be prudent to consult a labor law specialist.

The Resources

The Equal Employment Opportunity Commission (EEOC) has specific information about the rights of older workers under the Older Workers' Benefits Protection Act (OWBPA). Visit *www.eeoc.gov* for more information.

Avoiding Litigation

Prevention of Lawsuits

Without a doubt, employee-related litigation is the most prevalent type of litigation faced by small businesses. Avoiding litigation throughout the firing process is obviously beneficial to a company's bottom line. Other reasons to avoid litigation center around the lost productivity that normally occurs during a trial due to managers and employees being distracted from their jobs. Public relations and employee relations may also suffer if you become a company known for frequent employee litigation.

Lawsuits result throughout the process of involuntary termination when an employee feels that he or she is being discriminated against, treated inconsistently, or that the employer is out to get them.

The following 10 rules should be applied consistently during terminations to avoid lawsuits:

1. Never fire an employee on the spot, even if the offensive action or rule violation is an obvious reason for discharge. It is always best to suspend the employee pending further investigation.

2. Conduct a thorough, fully documented investigation of the facts leading to the potential decision to terminate. Have all employees involved in the incident–including the employee, witnesses, the supervisor, and human resources–sign a statement regarding what occurred.

3. Interview all employees involved in the incident, and reserve judgment until all the facts have been presented. Listen carefully to the employee and all witnesses, and be aware that union employees are entitled to have a representative of their choice accompany them to a disciplinary discussion.

4. Conduct the investigation promptly, immediately following the incident. The investigation should be completed within 48 to 72 hours of the event, and

the final decision should be made known to the employee within 24 to 48 hours afterward.

5. Have an unbiased third party conduct a final review of the facts before you decide to fire for cause. This person should be initially unfamiliar with the facts of the investigation, and should ideally be a higher ranking company official or perhaps a lawyer.

6. Be specific on the reason(s) for discharge, and make sure that you have verifiable proof. Refer in writing to work rules, policies, or the employee handbook whenever possible. Complete documentation is essential, not only in avoiding litigation but in defending the company should litigation occur.

7. Inform the employee of the company's decision to fire them in person. It is also advisable to have a second company representative in the room during the firing process. This is a time to ensure that the employee being fired is treated humanely and respectfully, and to prevent parting on bad terms. Issue the employee's final paycheck, if possible, and explain his or her rights under COBRA. Treat the exiting employee professionally throughout the firing process.

8. The use of progressive discipline is advisable when appropriate, because it demonstrates the company's intention to correct the errant behavior or performance that leads to termination. Consistency and documentation are essential when using progressive discipline.

9. Once you have determined that firing the employee is justified, do not delay. Employees do not usually fire themselves, so avoid procrastinating over your final decision or be intimidated by the fear of a lawsuit.

10. An employee who knows that he or she is close to being fired may try to get you to do or say something illegal, so that they can sue and possibly collect a settlement. Avoid this trap. If you have abided by the law, acted in good faith and in a nondiscriminatory manner, and followed company rules and policies, then you have the advantage should the employee bring a lawsuit against you.

Company Practices and Policies

Companies can avoid litigation by being proactive, even before an employee considers bringing a lawsuit. Take these proactive steps to prevent legal action.

Interviewer Training

Ensure that those responsible for hiring are skilled interviewers, so they can identify and hire qualified employees from the start. If your turnover rate is

too high, consider the possibility that your interviewers may be
poorly prepared.

Employee Handbooks

When company policies and procedures are documented in an employee
handbook, employees should understand what is expected of them. If a
violation occurs, company representatives can readily refer to those policies
and procedures to decide whether to proceed with a disciplinary action.

Performance Appraisals and Evaluations

Companies with documented employee appraisal and performance
evaluations give employees ample opportunity to improve where necessary.
Those employees who are fired for lack of performance should not be
surprised by the decision, as their performance is usually well documented.

Management Training

Managers and supervisors should know the company rules, applicable
discrimination laws, and what constitutes a wrongful discharge. All
managers should be up to speed on all rules, laws and documentation
practices. Managers in union shops should be well versed in their collective
bargaining agreements.

Communication

An important element in avoiding litigation is good communication
between supervisors and employees. In many cases, a situation might have
been resolved if both parties met and listened to each other; without this
intervention, a minor situation escalates into an unresolved conflict and often
leads to termination and litigation. It helps to have a knowledgeable human
resources advisor to counsel management so they can comply with current
labor law during difficult employee interactions.

Negotiation

Egos can get in the way of sound judgment if a termination meeting escalates.
Artful negotiation of settlement terms, however, can be a win-win situation for
both sides.

Mediation

Have an unbiased third party meet together with both sides, and attempt to
reach a mutually satisfactory agreement. While mediation is not binding, it is
often a beneficial alternative to litigation.

Arbitration

A professional arbitrator meets with both sides, hears the facts of the dispute,
and issues a decision. Arbitration differs from mediation in that the final
decision is binding. Arbitration clauses are frequently included in contracts as
a way to stay out of the courts.

Employment Contracts

Carefully written contracts can often dissuade a terminated employee from suing the company. Where a contract specifies employment at-will status, a terminated employee will likely avoid going to trial. This is an alternative, but it is still safer to fire for just cause.

Severance Package

An employee who is offered severance may opt to avoid litigation. In such cases, the employer will usually have the outgoing employee sign a statement indicating that they will not bring a lawsuit in the future.

There are no guarantees that an employee who is being fired will not later sue you. The best way for companies to avoid litigation during the firing process is to know the applicable laws, abide by them, act in fairness and in good faith, and document every step of the way.

The Resources

Visit the following Websites for articles related to avoiding litigation:

How to Avoid Lawsuits by Carlotta Roberts, *www.enterpreneur.com.*

Cardinal Rules of Termination by Francis T. Coleman, *www.shrm.org.*

Common Sense Tips For Avoiding Litigation by Brit Brown, *www.library.findlaw.com.*

Providing References for Terminated Employees

How Much Should I Say?

When asked to provide a reference for a terminated employee, how much information should you give? Any company that has fired an employee must address this issue. It is not uncommon for a discharged employee to request a reference from his or her former company. Deciding whether to give a reference is a dilemma for many organizations, mostly because of the fear of becoming entangled into a lawsuit. If you provide too much information about a former employee or interject factual statements with opinions that go beyond what the new employer asked, you could run a high risk of being sued for defamation or invasion of privacy. On the other hand, if you are omit important facts or provide false information, a defamation claim may also result. Where is the middle ground? Here are some ideas to help you decide.

Employers who are asked to give a reference for a former, or soon to be former, employee generally follow one of seven policies:

1. Tell Everything

    The employer openly discusses all issues pertaining to the employee, good and bad.

2. If You Do Not Have Something Nice to Say, Do Not Say Anything At All

    The employer provides a recommendation for good employees, but refuses to give references for bad employees.

3. No Comment

    The former employer provides no information at all.

4. Name, Rank and Title

    The employer confirms employment and provides only the dates of hire and termination, starting and ending salaries and position held.

5. I Have No Idea What to Do

    The employer has no specific policy; responses vary depending upon who is seeking the information, who is providing it, whether the person providing the information is in a giving or ugly mood or perhaps, is not qualified to give the reference at all.

6. I will only answer the questions I am asked
The employer will offer no information and only provides monosyllabic answers: yes, no, or good.

7. Reference Letter
The employer provide a short reference letter confirming employment and including a sentence or two about the employee's work; the company will not answer any questions except to verify that the letter is authentic.

These are all workable approaches, but from a potential liability perspective, the safest approaches are the No Comment policy and the Name, Rank, and Title policy. It is safe to say that employers who adopt such policies reduce their risk of liability.

The obvious problem with no-comment referral is that it completely undermines the purpose and value of a referral. A neutral reference denies a good employee the benefits of the employee's positive work history. By the same token, a neutral referral gives an unfair advantage to poor employees who, aware that nothing negative will be said about them when they seek their next job, have less incentive to do good work.

A recent ruling handed down by the New Mexico Court of Appeals acknowledges that employers have a right to refuse to give any information at all, without fear of liability. This ruling makes it perfectly legal for a company to not provide any type of reference, positive or negative.

While the ruling may shield companies from legal action, it allows companies to restrict the amount of information provided to employers about prospective employees. This may mean that less qualified workers might get jobs that more qualified applicants would have been offered if full information had been disclosed. It may also mean that applicants who are not good candidates for a particular position might land positions that are beyond their skill sets.

Withholding information may expose an employer to third-party liability. If the reasons for termination involved fraud, theft, violence, or some other form of illegal or egregious behavior, you could be held liable for failure to disclose this information to a future employer when called for a reference—even if your company policy does not allow detailed references. For example, if a new employer requests a reference from a former employer, the former employer does not disclose the employee's dangerous behavior, and the employee later causes injury to other employees or property, the former employer may be liable. In these situations, consult with an attorney before providing an employment reference.

There are, however, times when providing only a limited reference can harm a good employee's changes at landing a new job. Such an instance would be if an employee is discharged for reasons other than poor performance or unacceptable conduct–such as lack of work or the company's need for a different skill set. The new company would not be able to verify the reason for the discharge and may pass over this candidate for the position.

If you choose to provide references, be sure your policy is consistent for every employee. Here are additional items to include in your reference policy:

- Provide a reference release form for employees to sign upon leaving the organization, one that releases you from any liability for responding truthfully to any questions asked during the reference request. Notify departing employees that without a signed release, your company will provide name, rank and title references only.

- Assign a point person within your organization who will be responsible for handling all reference inquiries. Instruct other employees not to provide any information, but to direct all reference calls or letters to this individual. Make sure the designated person is trained properly to provide reference information.

- An employee cannot win a defamation suit unless the reference provides intentionally false information. Provide only honest information and express opinions as opinions rather than statements of fact. Do not respond with malice. Limit the information given to the employee's job-related performance. Do not divulge gossip or personal information, such as an individual's medical condition, political beliefs or religious practices. Do not provide unsolicited information; address only the specific questions asked.

- Verify the identity of the person requesting the reference. Make sure that the person is an appropriate individual to be receiving the information and that the former employee knows that his or her references are being checked. If in doubt about the identity of the person requesting the reference, ask for the request in writing on company letterhead, and then follow up with a verification phone call. Never give out any information to parties that do not have a legitimate need to know.

- Communicate the policy to all employees and indicate that it will be strictly followed.

Keep in mind that just as your company wants to learn as much as possible about a prospective worker before extending an offer, other employers want to gain knowledge as well. Courts are now recognizing that employers have a legitimate need to exchange performance-related information, and they increasingly protect companies that choose to provide more detailed employment references, as long as employers provide information that is job-related, based on reasonable evidence, and without malice.

Additional legislation passed in 2005 shields employers from liability for providing job references, unless the information they provide is knowingly false, deliberately misleading, or made with reckless disregard for the truth. Under this legislation, an employer will be presumed to have provided a job reference in good faith and shall be entitled to immunity if (1) the information is provided at the request of another employer or employment agency and (2) the disclosed information relates to:

- The employee's ability to perform his or her job;
- the employee's diligence, skill, or reliability in carrying out job duties; or
- illegal or wrongful acts committed by the employee when related to job duties.

The presumption of good faith may be disputed by clear and convincing evidence that the information disclosed was knowingly false, deliberately misleading, or made with a reckless disregard for the truth. The statute advises that employers should keep a written record of the identity of persons or entities to which the disclosure is made for a minimum of 2 years from the date of the disclosure. However, if such a record is kept, it must be included in the employee's personnel file, which the employee has the right to inspect.

Under Title VII, it is illegal for an employer to give a bad reference for a former employee in retaliation for the employee filing a discrimination claim.

The Resources

An excellent source for more information on the topic of providing references, visit CCH's *Ask Alice* feature for small businesses at *www.toolkit.cch.com*. This Website is generally very useful and friendly with solid information.

Jill Blackmer article, *Employee References: Can an Employer Ever Win?* is a useful and concise statement of the problem in providing references. Visit *www.meritas.org* for further information.

Resources

This section is devoted exclusively to resources–books, seminars, Internet sites and more–with additional information on the proper ways to hire and fire on behalf of your organization.

Websites

Nightingale Conant sells audio products on a variety of business and personal topics, including motivation and negotiations. Visit *www.nightingale.com* for details.

You can purchase a *Hiring Policy Kit*, which includes policies, forms and standard letters, at *www.hrpolicyanswers.com*.

Employment forms can be obtained from Websites such as *www.socrates.com*, *www.findlaw.com* and *www.lawdepot.com*.

Commerce Clearing House, a major legal and business publisher of topical reports and reference works, provides a wealth of employment-related information at *www.toolkit.cch.com*.

Your federal tax dollars help to educate companies on labor laws and regulations. Visit the Websites of the Department of Labor (*www.dol.gov*) and the Equal Employment Opportunity Commission (*www.eeoc.gov*) for information on ensuring proper compliance with these laws.

The Website *www.humancapitalinstitute.org* features a webcast series about on-Boarding at no cost.

In the event that you need to hire an attorney, *www.martindale.com* can help you locate a labor lawyer who specializes in your particular area of need.

A presentation at *www.dol.gov/asp/programs/drugs/said/StateLaws.asp* lists those state regulations concerning drug testing.

Books and Newsletters

An excellent, general law reference book is the *Socrates Practical Law Handbook: Solutions for Everyday Legal Questions* (Socrates Media, 2006). This book contains a section on employment law, and is generally helpful for both business and personal needs.

The National Institute of Business Management at *www.nibm.net* offers informative newsletters, downloads and monographs on a variety of business subjects, including hiring and firing.

*The Complete Reference Checking Handbook: Smart, Fast, Legal Ways to Check out Job Applicant*s (Amacom, 1998) is an fine source that details the process of checking references. Visit *www.amazon.com* or other online booksellers to purchase this book.

Seminars

Should you be interested in attending a seminar or training session to improve and expand your hiring and firing skills, visit *www.seminarinformation.com.* This Website is a clearinghouse for established business education groups. The Website's Quicksearch feature allows you to type in a subject and locate seminars in your area.

You can search for seminars on many business topics at *www.skillpath.com* and *www.amanet.org* (the latter has five regional training centers: New York, Chicago, Washington D.C., Atlanta and San Francisco).

Index

401(k) 20, 134

A

academic credentials 62
accommodation 10, 11, 12, 107,
    108
ad
  classified 25, 26, 39
  display 25
  Internet 31
  magazine 25
  newspaper 25, 26, 27, 28
  adverse action 61, 62
  affirmative action 109, 110, 112
  age discrimination 57, 110, 111,
    113, 114, 115, 117, 123, 129
Age Discrimination in Employment
  Act (ADEA) 57, 110, 113, 115,
    117, 123, 129
agreement
  collective 158
  employment 71, 81, 83, 130, 131,
    162, 199
  non-compete 82, 83, 84
  non-disclosure 81, 83, 84
allowance
  job search 155
  relocation 132
Alternative Trade Adjustment
  Assistance (ATAA) 153, 154

Americans with Disabilities Act of
    1990 (ADA) 10, 11, 14, 105,
    106, 107, 108, 110, 118, 123,
    129
Architectural/Transportation Tax
    Deduction 108

B

benchmarking 5, 15
best practice 4, 5, 6
bona fide occupational qualification
    (BFOQ) 58, 113
branding
  competitors' 34
  employment 33, 36
  plan 34, 35
Bureau of Labor Statistics (BLS) 16,
    121, 153, 156
business case 162

C

Civil Service Reform Act (CSRA) 124,
    129
compensation 10, 11, 15, 19, 45,
    46, 71, 73, 79, 89, 90, 91, 92,
    98, 106, 112, 117, 130, 132,
    134, 201
Consolidated Omnibus Budget
    Reconciliation Act of 1985
    (COBRA) 118, 119, 182, 199, 204
constructive discharge 160